I0109696

HOW TO MASTER THE ART OF SELLING 2

Winning the Game of Sales

HOW TO MASTER THE ART OF SELLING 2

Winning the Game of Sales

Taylor McCarthy

Foreword by Tom Hopkins

This publication is designed to provide competent and reliable information regarding the subject matter covered. However, it is sold with the understanding that the authors and publisher are not engaged in rendering legal, financial, or other professional advice. Laws and practices vary from state to state, country to country, and if legal or other expert assistance is required, the services of a professional should be sought. The authors and publisher specifically disclaim any liability that is incurred from the use or application of the contents of this book.

Made for Success Publishing
www.MadeForSuccess.com

Distributed by Made for Success

First Printing

Library of Congress Cataloging-in-Publication data
Author McCarthy, Taylor
How to Master the Art of Selling 2: Winning the Game of Sales
p. cm.

LCCN: 2025950952
ISBN: 978-1-64146-981-4 *(Hardcover)*
ISBN: 978-1-64146-983-8 *(eBook)*
ISBN: 978-1-64146-982-1 *(Audio)*

Printed in the United States of America

For further information, contact Made for Success Publishing
email service@madeforsuccess.net

To my father, Timothy McCarthy,
who made me the man I am today.

ACKNOWLEDGMENTS

SO MANY PEOPLE have been instrumental in my ongoing journey to become the best version of myself while helping others along the way. I remember starting in door-to-door sales while still in high school, thanks to my brother Nathan, who set an example for me right from the beginning. He taught me that sales is a sport and that losing is never an option. Thank you, Nathan, for being a great brother and the pioneer who introduced me to a career in sales.

To my mentor, Tom Hopkins, for always believing in me and opening so many opportunities, from traveling to China to presenting in front of thousands of sales professionals, and for your trust and confidence to write the sequel to the greatest sales book of all time.

To my manager, Chris Munizzi, for believing in me and always having my back.

To all my students, this is my gift to you: "The secret to living is giving."

To all the families I have served and helped over the past eighteen years.

To door-to-door sales professionals, 99 percent of people can't do this. What it has taught me is worth its weight in gold.

CONTENTS

FOREWORD

OVER ONE HUNDRED years ago, Thomas J. Watson was the driving force behind what would become one of the largest companies in the world, IBM. He, like so many of even today's CEOs, worked in sales early in his career. His sales career was notoriously successful because of his personal belief that no one should ever stop training. He was constantly on the alert for new ways of selling, better ways of communicating with buyers, and ideas for product development. His famous slogan, "THINK," is still very much a part of IBM's innovative success. By "THINK," Watson meant to "take everything into consideration." Don't accept things as they are or at face value if it's your intention to excel.

In my five decades of teaching millions of sales professionals worldwide, I have never met anyone who embodies the everlasting values of Thomas J. Watson like Taylor McCarthy. Since entering the field of sales at age eighteen, Taylor has never stopped learning for his own personal development. He analyzes every aspect of his sales process, his communication skills, and how he can successfully relate to others. His belief is that "training eliminates trying." And I just love that!

The proof is in the pudding. Taylor's sales records are second to none, especially in his initial chosen path, the door-to-door sales industry. See the About the Author section in the back of the book for details about his success.

Taylor began selling door-to-door while still in high school. Talk about taking on a tough job! You get more doors slammed in your face in that type of selling than any other. Most teenagers wouldn't be able to handle the rejection. However, Taylor had the grit and determination to succeed despite the many rejections he faced. He decided to use those slammed doors as motivators.

I did the same back when knocking on doors was the thing to do in real estate. My thinking was, "If I have to do it anyway, I might as well make a game of it." Little did I know then that decades into the future, I'd meet someone else with the same philosophy and level of determination to succeed.

When I met Taylor in 2015, I was so impressed with his story of success with my sales training that I invited him, as I often do with successful students, to tell his story from the stage at one of my seminars. Mind you, by this point in my career, I had already taught multiple generations of salespeople. Having Taylor speak about the value of my training to him at age twenty-five, as I was considering wrapping up my own career, felt providential.

Being on the road as many days each year as I had puts a lot of wear and tear on you and your loved ones. When interviewers, long-time students, and even my staff were asking, "What's next?" I knew I had to find someone to carry my legacy of training into the future, or I'd never be able to ease my grueling schedule. I had long been on the lookout for someone with a similar heart and passion for training. Many attendees of my training would come up to me and tell me they were "going to be the next Tom Hopkins." I always encouraged them and asked them to stay in touch, knowing our time on earth has its limitations.

When Taylor not only stayed in touch but shared with me how he took my training to the next level, my belief in him grew exponentially. My conversations with him felt similar to the ones I had with my own mentor, J. Douglas Edwards, but with me on Mr. Edwards's side. Not only was Taylor continuing to excel in sales, but like me, he was being asked to teach and train others. He came to me asking for advice on how to develop his public speaking skills—like I did with Mr. Edwards. He asked my team for advice on study materials for *his* students. He wasn't trying to compete with me. He wanted to complement the work I had done.

Ever cautious about who to trust with the legacy of my training and that of Mr. Edwards, I found, in Taylor, exactly what I hoped to find. He has the drive, integrity, energy, and intelligence to carry the message of sales professionalism forward while enhancing the proven-effective tactics and strategies that have helped literally millions of sales professionals around the world to have life-changing careers. I fully expect his sales training career to exceed what I have accomplished.

Through our mutual love and respect for the profession, a great friendship has developed, and I am honored to pass the training gavel to Taylor McCarthy as the embodiment of the next generation of professional selling. I am grateful for him and admire his future plans.

I also cannot express how grateful I am that you are reading this book. I cannot encourage you enough to follow through with implementing Taylor's experience and wisdom into your own sales career. I've taught sales professionals for decades to eliminate the word "deal" from their sales vocabulary, and I still highly recommend it when communicating with clients, but I must break my own code by telling you that Taylor McCarthy is "the real deal." The content of this book proves it. He *will* help you achieve your goals and greatness.

When you seek wisdom, you want to get it from someone who has already accomplished what you want to achieve. Taylor has "been there," yet continues to go deep into the trenches of selling. His tactics and strategies are what you have been looking for. Don't just read this book. It's a textbook. Invest the time necessary to internalize the concepts so you can use them to serve yourself and others in the most beneficial way in this wonderful field of sales. Now, turn the page and start learning!

Tom Hopkins
Best-selling author,
How to Master the Art of Selling

CHAPTER 1

What is a Salesperson, and Why Were We Mislabeled from Day One?

THROUGHOUT THIS BOOK, I'm going to challenge you to think differently—differently about sales and differently about yourself. The reason for this comes from my own experience.

My parents divorced when I was twelve years old. My sister and I lived with our dad. Due to some serious health issues, he struggled to pay the bills and provide for us. It was hard for my younger self to watch. Most of the time, after the basics were covered, he was down to his last twenty dollars. There weren't many funds available for fun activities. I couldn't wait to start working so I wouldn't have to live like that much longer.

For reasons we don't need to get into, I wasn't a great student. In high school, I had a 1.8 GPA. I was more interested in getting on with life than learning what the school system said I needed to know. My personal education began on the golf course. As a teenager, I got a job as a golf caddy at the most prestigious course in Massachusetts. I learned how to talk with the golfers and, more importantly, when not to talk. I saw how much of golf was a mental game. I took it all in, and I hustled. I could carry two bags and often did. This earned me double the tips. As we reached the turn in the course, I would put my name back on the list to caddy another foursome. I could go right back out rather than having downtime. My desire and ability to hustle earned me significantly more money than the other caddies.

In my senior year, at eighteen, I got a job in door-to-door sales. I left school at midday and knocked on doors to sell TV, phone, and internet packages. You can imagine how many doors were never opened or slammed in my face. Not many people responded positively to a kid coming to their home to sell something. In today's ever-cautious world, you'd probably think I was casing your home for a potential home invasion.

For me, every closed door became a motivator. Rather than being discouraged, I became energized by every slam or quick "No, thanks." I learned to love rejection. I would tell myself, "Some do. Some don't. So what? Someone's waiting." I just had to keep going to find people who *were* interested in what I was selling.

To this day, I am still motivated by rejection. I am genuinely amused by hostile people. I view their reaction as a challenge. It challenges me to find the right approach to turn their negative feelings about me as a salesperson into something positive, to help them like me and earn their trust.

One day, I was doing field training with five top recruits in the solar industry. These people were already successful in door-to-door sales, earning around $80,000 per year. My goal was to teach them how to make it to the next level. Obviously, they already had some good techniques and strategies, but there is always more to learn.

That day, our designated work area was a gated community. Generally, soliciting is not allowed without permission from the Homeowners Association (HOA) or management company. What you need to do is collaborate with existing residents who might be willing to refer you to neighbors. The first sale is crucial. On the way to the location, I made up a story for the recruits to set the stage. It went something like this: "We are going to a home where the wife is upset about the high electric bill. She's frustrated with the amount of time her husband spends playing video games. We will give them a perfect presentation, and they'll be excited to own our product." They listened, but I doubted they understood my intention.

At the first door, a man answered. He saw me standing there and said, "This is a gated community." He slammed the door in my face.

I turned to the team and said, "That was the best ever! I will give his product to the neighbor." I smiled my biggest smile and turned toward the next house. I bounced on the balls of my feet with anticipation and energy for what was next door.

I knocked. The homeowner answered and, before I could say anything, slammed the door. I laughed out loud as I turned away and said, "That was fire! I'm having the best day of my life!" I'm sure the team thought I was crazy. I kept that same high energy as I walked to the third home. There, I found a woman who was very interested in my product. She let me in. I gave my best presentation, and she decided to go ahead. Then, she walked me over to her neighbor's house, made an introduction, talked about how she just purchased my product, and said they should hear me out. I made that sale, too.

When leaving the second home, I spotted another neighbor out watering their flowers. Now, my energy was contagious. I was able to tell that neighbor about the decision the other two had made and, you guessed it, made a third sale.

The team came to understand that my energy and expectations being the same at every door was my "secret sauce." I may not have a PhD in anything, but I have PMA—a Positive Mental Attitude. I did not let the actions of the first two homeowners put a dent in my energy for the rest. I kept my focus on sharing my enthusiasm and creating feelings of ownership in the homeowners. I did not hang onto the rejections or take them personally.

When you think of ways to create positive feelings in others, your creativity gets stimulated. You become other-focused. You stretch your mind to find the words that create a feeling in your buyers. That feeling creates a judgment. That judgment about you and your product brings about the decision.

In sales, this decision is known as "closing." I like to think of it as "creating feelings of ownership." When we are closing sales, we are creating feelings that generate opportunities for people to make decisions. That's the basis of a salesperson—someone who helps create positive opportunities for others to make their lives or their businesses better.

Salespeople Were Mislabeled

The simplest and most typical definition of a salesperson goes something like this: a person whose job is to sell a product or service. Let's break that down.

- Sales is a job. The absolute nature of a job is to get paid. Do it better than someone else, and you might expect to be paid better than that person or, at least, earn more for closing more sales than others.
- To sell means to exchange something for money. Sounds kind of impersonal, doesn't it? It can also mean to persuade. This leads most of the public to react as if we are trying to push something on them or convince them of something through coercion or manipulation.

If you and I went to the grocery store and asked random strangers what they thought of salespeople, what do you think they would say? Sleazy? Aggressive? Manipulative? That's how Hollywood portrays salespeople in the movies. Unfortunately, that's how some people in sales operate. And that is why 96 percent of the general population does not like salespeople.

When I ask *you* what you think of salespeople, what comes to mind? Hopefully, things like problem solver, educator, and maybe even persuader. If so, great. If not, I'm glad you are reading this book. Sales are what make the world go 'round. Imagine if there were no such thing as a sales job? What would you do for a living? More importantly, how would you, or anyone you know, learn about and purchase goods and services that make life and business better? Of course, a large number of sales occur online without salespeople. Consumers can easily access product details, specifications, and in-depth reviews. However, the internet hasn't entirely eliminated the need for salespeople, especially in the retail environment, business-to-business sales, and, of course, door-to-door sales. Those are the areas we will cover in this book.

Here's the thing: my primary goal in life is to help you and all salespeople start thinking of yourselves and the profession differently—to improve your attitude and image of the sales professional so you can serve more clients and earn a greater income. The bottom line? Let's help you have a more satisfying life through the field of selling.

It's my firm belief that salespeople have earned a bad rap. We should never have been called "salespeople." It is misleading because we don't just exchange goods and services for money. At the most basic level, that may be what happens, but that takes the human aspect out of the experience. It takes the emotion out of the equation. I believe human beings are the most emotional creatures on the planet. Everything we do has an emotion attached to it. Every word we hear creates pictures in our minds or generates a response. When we think about the communication skills required to create an emotional response in a buyer, there is a shift in approach in every aspect of what we do.

Think about it. Nobody wants to be "sold," but everyone wants to "own the benefits" of the various products they choose to bring into their lives, benefits like fun, security, and peace of mind. They want to acquire things that make them feel good. They want to get involved with services that make their lives easier or more fun. They want products that improve the bottom line of their businesses.

The primary role of salespeople is to make people feel comfortable learning about new products, ideas, and ways to enhance their lives or businesses. As sales professionals, we provide "a convenience." We bring buyers something that makes them feel better, do better, or have things easier. Sales are all about the feelings, not the transaction.

So, what should we have been called?

I strongly believe we should have been labeled "servants," "servicing professionals," or even "assistant buyers."

By definition, "servants" are people "working in the service of others." A servant's job is to make the lives of those they serve better and more comfortable. That's us! We are in the business of serving. We serve them by introducing them to better versions of something they already own or something entirely new that sparks their interest. We help them recognize challenges and educate them on opportunities to resolve them.

In the role of a servant, our number one goal is always to help buyers feel understood. We help them make sense of new knowledge, so they feel comfortable making decisions that will improve their lives, businesses, or the lives of their loved ones. In essence, we are helping people feel seen. It's like we're saying to them, "I see you. I see the need you have. I see that you are facing a challenge. I know how to make it better. So please, let me serve you."

Starting today, stop labeling yourself as a salesperson. I know it may say that on your business card, and that's between you and your company. You may have to abide by what they deem appropriate. However, you *can* change your *thinking* about what you do. Change your thinking about the job itself, and the job will change.

You are a servant. You are in the business of serving buyers. You are a teacher. You are in the business of educating buyers, helping people understand how their needs can be met and their lives improved. You are an assistant buyer. You are helping others find solutions and make wise decisions. Doesn't that feel better than thinking of yourself as a "salesperson?"

I do this type of work because I genuinely want to help others. I shifted my mindset to serve, not to get a paid commission. When you adopt an attitude like that, you never "work" a day in your life.

Depending on the product, service, or idea you are selling, you may be convening, or bringing together, ideas and people. You're not "selling" them. You're creating incredible, often exciting opportunities for the benefit of others.

I like to think of us as assistant buyers. We take the hands of our buyers and guide them through the decision process to their benefit. The words "to their benefit" are the key point here. If you don't believe 100 percent that your product or service is of more benefit to others than your commission is to you, you may have accepted the Hollywood stereotype of what you do for a living.

How we define ourselves is what makes the difference in the level of professionalism we demonstrate. Retitling job positions alters the perspective of every job. Not sure about that? How does your perception change between thinking of the person who picks up your weekly trash as a "garbage collector" versus a "sanitation worker"? The first might be viewed as picking up your smelly or useless discards. The other keeps your environment clean. Interesting, isn't it? How about "cop" versus "public safety officer"? One might be viewed as the enemy who gives out speeding tickets and holds up traffic; the other might be a hero who is first on the scene at an accident and saves lives with quick action.

If you're like most people, the level of respect you have for those revised titles improves. Same job, different perspective. So, let's work on increasing the level of respect we have for *our* jobs and the perspective others have of our profession. Creating that altered perception only takes a bit of practice. Let's begin with our own perspective.

The Practicing Professional

To become great at selling, start thinking of yourself as a "practicing professional." There's a common denominator with any professional, and that's the word "practice." A lawyer calls his work a practice. He or she is a "practicing" professional. The dentist has a practice. Same for doctors. They are considered professionals due to the level of education required to get and maintain their licenses, as well as the impact of the services they provide.

My question to you is this: If I wanted to be a doctor, could I attend college, graduate, and start earning $300,000 a year immediately? The answer is no. Even with the degree and license, I would have to do a residency, working with someone who is already a "practicing professional," to gain knowledge beyond what was in those medical textbooks. Doctors and lawyers invest a tremendous amount of time and energy, after they complete their education, in honing their craft. They pay the price at the beginning of their careers to reap the rewards later.

Sales are different in that getting into sales doesn't require a high level of education. I believe that's part of its appeal. You can get into the field with absolutely no experience. You don't have to pay tuition to learn the ropes. There are no licenses or certifications required, unless you're in the fields of real estate, financial services, or something similar. Anyone can get into sales. Staying in sales is the tricky part. If you're not earning a livable income, you won't want to stay in the field. If you're not making enough sales, the company won't want you to stay either. There is a risk involved that you must be willing to accept.

Some might think a downside of selling is that you learn most of your skills on the job. However, I see this as the most significant advantage. My level of education in sales is 100 percent dependent on me. My success is truly in my hands. The secret to success in this field is to never stop training, never stop looking for better ways to communicate with others—to create those feelings within them that cause them to decide to go ahead and own your offering. I continue to improve my skills as an assistant buyer and a practicing sales professional to this day. I strongly encourage you to do the same.

Some people think training is hard. I believe that not training makes your life harder. Training eliminates trying. When you make training a habit, it becomes easy. Your mind is always open to new ideas. You don't even think about it anymore. Some days, it seems that new ideas for better communication flow because you have chosen to become a practicing sales professional and assist buyers in making informed decisions.

So, let's give serious, conscious thought to how we think about ourselves and our selling career. Let's actively become practicing sales professionals so we can serve our clients better every day.

CHAPTER 2

Observation and Analysis

I WAS FORTUNATE to discover Tom Hopkins's training early in my career. Tom has been known for decades as the world's number one sales trainer. For years, he has toured both nationally and internationally, training well over five million sales professionals worldwide. His books have sold millions of copies. When his audio recordings were only available on cassette tape, top sales professionals were known to wear out copies by playing them over and over. Fortunately for me, his recordings became available on CDs, then as MP3s.

I started listening to Tom's recordings in 2008. He taught me not to come across as that stereotypical salesperson we've all heard about. He raised my awareness so much that I analyzed every aspect of myself, how I present myself in the world, and the words I use with buyers. I did everything he suggested and more. It made all the difference in the foundation of my personal development and my success as a practicing sales professional and trainer.

My sales record of earning three back-to-back number one sales awards in the alarm industry connected me with Tom Hopkins on a personal level. I sent him a message, sharing what I accomplished with the help of his training, and he reached out to me by phone. There I was, age twenty-four, taking a call from someone whom I idolized. I was nervous about what to say to him and floored when he invited me to a seminar in California to tell my story to his audience.

As Tom prepared me for my time on stage, I asked him about the best advice he had ever received. He shared a message he received from *his* mentor before starting his speaking career: always give more than your audience expects.

His words have inspired me to do the same when selling products and providing training to clients. I have now developed even more tactics and strategies beyond what I learned from him, as I live and breathe above and beyond "sales" and "service." To top it all, Tom and I have become very close, even doing some training together.

The Value of Observation

One of the most valuable skills I have developed is to be highly observant of my surroundings. I am constantly on the lookout for clues about potential buyers, including where they live, the types of homes they own, whether they have children, the types of vehicles they drive, and even their landscaping. As those clues tell me about them, I constantly analyze how I might best approach them to earn their respect and trust. I'm always asking myself, "How can I connect with them to make them comfortable with me?" I seek ways to "tune in to their frequency."

A good example of this is to think about radio stations. If you are listening to a station on the 94.5 frequency, it may be perfectly clear. But what happens if you are just one or two digits off, say on 94.4 or 94.6? You're likely to hear garbled words and static, right? When you are not speaking at the right frequency for your potential buyers, they will not hear you clearly. There may even be a disconnect between the message you think you are delivering and what they are interpreting. With great observation skills, you are equipped to quickly make adjustments to speak at their frequency, to be heard clearly.

It's the same in business sales. Using your powers of observation, take in things such as the type and quality of clothing a buyer wears, their jewelry, and the state of their office. If that's where you're meeting, note any photos on their desks or walls, or any other items that tell you about them personally or about their business. In essence, you are operating like a detective. These are all clues about what's important to them. Those clues are all potential icebreakers or conversation-starters. They help you gauge their "frequency." Communicating with buyers on topics of interest enhances the authentic human aspect of your communication, lessening the transactional aspects. It helps you develop trust and earn their respect.

To determine how good you are at matching frequencies, here are a few questions to consider:

1. How observant are you? When you are with buyers, are you focused on what you're going to say? Or are you paying more attention to what's important to them?

2. How do you think about what you encounter? How much value do you put on what you observe?

3. How do people react to your presence? Have you developed the skill of reading body language?

If you are not already confident in your answers to those questions, don't worry. I will share what I've found to be powerfully successful in each of those areas.

Once I started thinking about how to make the people I was contacting feel good about their time with me, I began adjusting my approach. I changed how I conversed with them. *I changed.*

I finally had something I felt was worth studying. I became an A-plus student of selling. It made all the difference in my life. It's also allowed me to make a positive difference in the lives of my loved ones, which is the most rewarding aspect of a successful sales career. More about that later.

Through observation, I became creative with what I said, my physical presence, and how I kept the focus on the buyer and their problems, needs, and solutions. For example, I am taller than the average American male. Because of that, I keep my distance when meeting people. I don't want to "tower over them" or force them to strain their necks to make eye contact, which might make them feel fearful. When selling door-to-door, the sooner I sit down with buyers, the better. It puts us on a more even level and allows us to be in closer proximity. The entire encounter feels more relaxed. Have you ever noticed this? If not, I encourage you to do so.

I am constantly on the lookout for ways to be innovative and creative and to improve as a sales professional.

Words Create Feelings

Every word used in sales either works for us or against us. This lesson is so important that I recommend re-reading that sentence until you have taken it to heart and start paying attention to *every word* you use with buyers. By the way, it's just as important to do this with loved ones and friends during all of your communications.

Because some words can have different meanings, they have the potential to generate a variety of images and feelings in the people you are trying to serve. You don't know which image or feeling they'll experience until you use them and observe the buyers' reactions. This can be the trickiest part of what sales professionals do. You have to develop your skills *and* your reflexes to adapt quickly. The more comfortable you can make buyers feel, the more sales you will close, and the more money you will make.

Have you ever noticed a change in your buyers' demeanor when you said something? I would be surprised if you answered "no" to this question. It's human nature to notice when a vibe changes. In sales, this shift occurs when the buyer's wall of resistance increases. They may even physically take a step back or lean back in their chair. You need to pay attention to these signs if you want to do business with them. It's a sign that you've said something that, in essence, gave them pause. You may even have inadvertently made them think of something that generated fear. Everything you say either helps or hurts the forward progress of the sale. There's no "neutral" when communicating with buyers.

The Basis of Fear

With the negative connotation around the title "salesperson," there is almost an instantaneous fear in buyers that we are going to try to get something over on them. It's sad, but true. We don't often begin with buyers on an even playing field. We may start in a pile of muck and mud based on their perception. This is especially true in consumer sales situations. We have to present ourselves as atypical immediately to lower their fears.

What is fear anyway? It's the greatest enemy of all. Most salespeople fear rejection. Buyers fear being sold something that won't turn out to be what they expect. Buyers also fear making the wrong decision. The best definition I've heard is this: False Evidence Appearing Real (FEAR). If fear is "false evidence," where does it come from? It boils down to fear being generated by something unknown, or known but negative.

When we encounter something unknown, our brains automatically try to make sense of it. This triggers our innate fight, flight, or freeze safety mechanism. You know the feeling. If it's truly unknown, the only way to get past it is to continue the encounter and make it known. This was J. Douglas Edwards's advice back in the early days of sales training. Known as the Father of Modern Selling, he said, "Do what you fear most, and you control fear." In other words, by making the unknown known, you gain power over your reaction to it. It really can be that simple.

Each step into the unknown lessens its effect on us. As practicing sales professionals, we help buyers do the same through the words we use. By sharing our product and industry knowledge with them, we eliminate that powerful fear driver: the unknown.

When a past negative experience causes fear, we use effective communication skills to help buyers acknowledge and rationalize their past experiences, becoming open to new ones that may very well turn out to be positive. We persuade them to give the situation a second chance. Nobody wants to make a wrong decision more than once. It feels awful, possibly even embarrassing.

Even when the new opportunity sounds great, most people's natural reaction is that it sounds too good to be true. They become skeptical, looking for the "catch" because they don't want to get taken advantage of. Our job becomes one of demonstrating our servant-ship. Show that you're on their side—the side of resolving a challenge with a powerful win.

When we can help people like us, they'll trust what we are saying. When they trust what we're saying, they become more open to considering what we offer. We must make our products or services make sense to them because a confused mind always says "no." When we help buyers see how much sense our product makes, fear and confusion become a non-factor. When we first meet buyers, it's typical for their anxiety about dealing with us to be high, and their certainty about us to be low. Our primary job is to alleviate their anxiety and increase their confidence. When that happens, we create opportunities for favorable decisions. Anxiety is the acid that wipes out your enthusiasm.

Let's revisit the idea that fear is created by what is "known, but negative" in the minds of our buyers. Negativity is a feeling, right? We'll talk more about creating an emotional climate for closing in a later chapter, but let's lay the foundation here first.

That cautious, "too good to be true" skepticism is likely triggered by something you say to the buyer. You may not even know which words they are until you increase your powers of observation. However, there are some words commonly used in sales that create negative feelings that you can eliminate right now.

Nasty Words and Their Replacements

This is one of my favorite topics because it's so simple to understand and implement. Changing your word choice with buyers is elementary but so powerful. This goes back to the question of perception between the "cop" and the "public safety officer." Everyone knows what they mean, but the feelings associated with them are different.

I first learned about this technique from my mentor, Tom Hopkins, and he learned it from his mentor, J. Douglas Edwards. They call these words to avoid "nasty words." Tom added to what he learned from Mr. Edwards, and I've come up with even more. The first words to eliminate from your vocabulary are "sell" and "sold." When you say, "Hey, I just sold this guy…" or when a buyer says, "Hey, I just got sold," it's just a nasty way of thinking. No one wants to "get sold." We want our buyers to "get involved with" our products and services. We want to "help them acquire" the benefits of our offerings.

I encourage you to practice using words that create a better mental picture as soon as possible and watch how buyers react differently to you. By utilizing the right vocabulary and asking the right questions, we demonstrate a higher level of professionalism, which helps buyers shift their certainty in our favor and lowers their anxiety and fear.

Feel the difference when we say, "I sold this to your friend, George," versus "When George got involved with this program, he was able to save money on a bill he had been dreading." The conversation is no longer about you, the sales guy, someone they may not like or trust. It's about the benefits received by a client of yours. The buyer can receive those same benefits when they decide to own your product. The focus is on the buyer "getting involved" or "acquiring," not on you selling. When you keep the focus of the conversation coming from the buyer's perspective, you create feelings of understanding and ownership. People are not going to do business with you because they understand what you're saying. They'll do business with you because they feel understood.

The next word to eliminate from your vocabulary is "buy." We all buy things all the time. There's little or no emotional involvement in picking up the weekly groceries or getting gas. Notice I said, "emotional involvement," not just "emotion." There can certainly be emotion around spending money on groceries and gas, especially when inflation is high. However, "emotional involvement" happens when there's a dopamine hit from being happy, fulfilled, or excited about making purchases. That happens when people truly want to "own" the benefits of what they're acquiring. Giving people the opportunity to experience "ownership"—that's a lot better than asking them to "buy" something.

Next is the word "deal." You might be thinking that the phrase "a good deal" is positive. However, once again, we've all gotten into "deals" that didn't turn out to be as good as expected. Also, again, there's that Hollywood portrayal of a "good deal" as not-so-good. What we do, as practicing professionals, is provide people with "opportunities" to "transact" or "get people involved" with our offering. We do not do "deals" with buyers. We have completed a certain number of "transactions." We help families "get involved with" the benefits of our products.

Another word to reconsider using in consumer sales is "appointment." Don't say, "Let's set an appointment for 10 a.m." Save that for the doctors, dentists, and lawyers. Salespeople who set "appointments" with consumers have high cancellation rates. Practicing sales professionals, instead, keep things casual and light. They get permission to "pop by and visit" when working with consumers. The inference here is that your meeting time will not interfere with their day. An "appointment" can feel more like a commitment, which can create that fear we are trying to avoid. In a business setting, suggest setting "a time to meet" versus an "appointment." It's more casual and more personal.

The sooner you stop using the word "payment" or "monthly payments," the better. No one wants more of them, including us. Replace those words with "amount" or "monthly investment." Saying, "The monthly amount would be X" rather than "The monthly payment would be X," mentally softens the blow of spending money. Change the mental picture.

One of the nastiest nasty words to use is "pitch." Nobody wants to be "pitched." A pitch is a baseball throw.

It's the angle of a roof. It's a soccer field in Europe. We do not "pitch" people. We "present." We give "presentations" where we ask the right questions to solve problems. We present problems, then we present solutions.

Next up is the word "sign." Using the word "sign" creates fear. What have we always been told about "signing" things? Don't do it! That word creates fear and causes hesitation. When you ask someone to "sign the contract," it can be even worse. Those words have the potential to bring your sales process to a screeching halt or trigger a negative response such as "I want to think it over." Starting today, ask people, instead, to "okay," "approve," or "authorize the paperwork." It feels different, doesn't it?

The word "contract" often causes people to make the decision bigger than it needs to be. Replacing "contract" with "form," "agreement," or "paperwork" that needs "approval" changes the entire feeling of the decision-making process.

There was an instance where one of my buyers told me, "I'm not signing any contracts today." Rather than assuming that was a final "no," I said, "Alright, we only need you to okay the forms so we can move to the next step." She visibly relaxed and "approved the paperwork," which allowed me to have my team take the next step of determining the specs related to her needs.

Your next nasty word is "customer." The reason I'm asking you to change this word goes back to our job being one of servant-ship. We need to think of "customers" as "the people we serve" and "the companies we serve." Using these terms keeps everything service-minded, which leads back to us behaving as assistant buyers.

Another word to stop using with the families or "people we serve" is "cheaper." No one really wants a cheaper product. The perception is that it may be cheaply made or of lesser quality. They DO want products that are "more economical" or "the most economical." Using these terms implies that our products will be a smarter purchase than going with our competition.

This next one is a pet peeve of mine. I cringe when I hear people use the phrase "to be honest." It's as if everything they said previously was not honest, maybe even that they were lying. Don't allow that perception to be created! Use the phrases "to be blunt" or "to be frank." "Sue, may I have your permission to be blunt with you?" The term "blunt" shows that I want to speak plainly and be straightforward with them. By making this change, I'm removing the likelihood that they will perceive me as someone with an ulterior motive. Instead, it's as if we're getting to the bottom line of our discussion, which is the only thing most people want to hear.

Your next nasty word is "commission." This word generates a question in the mind of your buyer: "What do *you* get out of this?" Or "Am I paying you above and beyond getting the product?" It takes their attention away from what *they* get by acquiring the benefits of your product. If a question about commission arises, be "frank" and let them know there *is* a "fee for service built into" the transaction. This changes the focus of the conversation to the amount or level of service they will receive. Keeping the focus on their benefits is critical to your overall success in selling.

The last in my current list of nasty words is "problem." Unless you want to use the word to emphasize the downside of a situation you are helping to fix, start using the term "challenge" instead. It's especially important to use "challenge" in your self-talk. Challenges, by definition, are more of a dare, a test of your skills and abilities—something to be overcome. For many, the word "problem" brings to mind a barricade, a reason to halt forward progress. The word "challenge" suggests a hurdle. It might slow you down or cause you to rethink your sprint to the finish line, but it's 100 percent possible to overcome one or work around it.

Glamour Words

Now, the opposite of what I call nasty words are glamour words. Glamour words are commonly known but uncommonly used words. They build curiosity and excitement during your presentations. These are typically adjectives that generate positive excitement around your offering. If you want to see some good examples of these, read the descriptions for new homes on the market. Winning real estate companies offer homes that are "bright and airy." They might have "high-end" upgrades. These adjectives are used purposely because they have proven effective.

Invest some time in reading the descriptive promotional information about your product that's on your company website or other sales material. Read it with an eye for how the description makes you feel. If you feel it's appropriate and effective, great! If not, consider the adjectives you might add to enhance the emotions buyers feel about your offerings.

As a practicing sales professional, when you become more attuned to your powers of observation, how others respond or react to what you say and do, you'll automatically become more adept at making course corrections with the words you use. Those course corrections equate to more effective skills in the areas of communication and persuasion, which result in a smoother sales process and more closed sales. And that's what we really want, isn't it?

CHAPTER 3

The Definition of Selling: The Art of Blending Complete Opposites

I LIKE TO break things down to the ridiculous. By that, I mean the most basic, simplest concepts. That's when lightbulbs go off in my head. That is when I gain the most precise understanding of what I want and need to do. I apply this strategy to everything.

Our job as assistant buyers is to make people feel comfortable both in recognizing their needs and in agreeing to solutions. Therefore, the two simplest elements of selling that we must rely on are these: communication and persuasion.

When it comes to communication, we've all heard the saying, "It's not what you say that matters; it's how you say it that counts." I disagree. There's more to it than that. What truly matters in communication is *how you make others feel.* As a sales professional, you can "communicate" all day long, but if your words and actions do not cause others to feel the need or desire to own your offering, it's an exercise in futility. This relates to Maya Angelou's most famous quote: "People will forget what you said, people will forget what you did, but people will never forget how you made them feel."

When it comes to persuasion, some people think that you're forcing something on someone that they may not really want. I see persuasion as simply asking the right questions to point out both a problem and a solution. While the problem and solution are opposites, when we blend our knowledge and skills to communicate those two opposites, we create opportunities for decisions to be made.

For that reason, I define sales as *the art of blending complete opposites.* When you develop this skill, your results will improve. I've proven this to be true, and so have thousands of the people I've taught. Let's get into some of those opposites.

Trust and Respect

Tom Hopkins taught me that my number one goal when meeting someone I could potentially serve was to help them "like me, trust me, and want to listen to me." If I didn't make all three happen, making a sale would be tough.

I worked hard on my approach to lower people's defenses and be "likable." That opened the door, so to speak, for them to want to hear what I had to say, but building trust was tougher, especially in my early days of selling as a teen. A lack of trust when trying to sell is like having a phone with no service plan. You can only play games on it. No real communication can happen.

I quickly learned that I had to earn respect AND build trust before I could get very far in the sales process. People just wouldn't listen if they didn't think they could trust me. Yet, if I earned 100 percent of their trust and they liked me, that didn't mean they were going to do business with me. I also needed to deepen their respect for me and how they perceived me as a professional.

In society, there's a basic level of respect that most human beings give to their fellow humans. Assumptions that determine how deep that respect will go are made starting the moment others lay eyes on us or first hear our voices. Judgments are being made about how we dress, how we speak, and our physical presence, such as our posture, stance, and movement. All this happens in just a few seconds, sometimes even before our first words register in their thoughts. If we don't earn respect by what we do and say, people won't believe that we will take proper care of them and their needs. Their defenses will go up, and our sales closings will go down.

People feel respected when they are heard and feel understood. Most people will respond respectfully when you demonstrate respect toward them. Being genuinely interested in and open to others strengthens relationships and builds trust.

Since the beginning of time, humans have held an innate wariness, or lack of trust, in anything new or different. This includes ideas, things, and other people. It's part of everyone's natural instinct to protect themselves. This lack of trust is the primary objection you will always face.

From the moment a potential buyer lays eyes on you, you need to communicate in a way that builds trust in you, in what you are saying, in your product, and in your company. They need to trust that they'll get the benefits you and your product promise to provide before any decisions can be made.

Think about your last visit to the doctor or dentist. Many people experience what is known as "white coat syndrome." They are simply afraid to go to the doctor, and doing so literally causes an increase in their blood pressure. So, what do smart, professional doctors do about it? Some simply don't wear white coats. But even before you see them, they may have done something to change your feelings about this experience. Is there a fish tank in the lobby? Are there plants similar to what you might have at home? Is the seating more like your living room and less like a bus station? Are the staff in regular clothing instead of scrubs? Is the television showing something soothing with relaxing music instead of medical information or the latest bad news?

There's a comedian whose skit includes a reference to fish tanks in doctors' waiting rooms. He says if there are goldfish in the tank, you probably don't want to take that doctor's advice. If the tank resembles something from an underwater diving experience, the doctor is likely more successful. He or she is actively trying to earn your trust.

We demonstrate that we are trustworthy through our words and actions. When we are truly practicing professionals, our communication skills are solid. Our conversations are not filled with what Tom Hopkins calls "seal talk." Seal talk is something we use to fill the blanks in conversations when our reflexes aren't strong enough or when we are nervous. They are words and phrases such as "um," "uh," "you know," and "like."

Another thing to avoid when communicating is what DJs call "dead air." Dead air is defined as a period of silence during a customer interaction when neither the customer nor the salesperson is communicating. Dead air is most often interpreted by buyers as you having a knowledge gap, and it's a trust killer. When we appear unsure of ourselves, others are less likely to trust what we say. When we speak with confidence, trust grows.

You may not believe that you use any seal talk or ever allow dead air. Most salespeople I meet feel that way. These flaws appear because our brains are working so hard to come up with the next few words that we don't even hear ourselves fill the gaps with "ums" and "ahs" or allow breaks in communication. I strongly encourage you to record yourself during a presentation or two. When you listen to the recording the first time, only listen for seal talk. Then, go back and listen for dead air. If you have any, determine the cause. Were you asked a question you couldn't answer? If so, get on it to find the answer so it doesn't happen again. With another listen, you can analyze the non-seal talk words and how effective they are in creating emotions in the buyer.

State Your Intentions

I find it extremely helpful to use an intent statement early in my sales process. An intent statement verbally sets the tone for your presentation and relieves pressure. It's especially useful during a first meeting with a buyer who isn't sure about you or your product. It goes like this: "Thank you for the time you're giving me. Please know that I will respect it. To present you only with the information relevant to you, I need to ask a few questions. May I have your permission to do that?" (Pause to allow them to answer.) "Thank you. I also want to mention that I'm a consumer myself, and I know my product isn't right for everyone. I want to put your mind at ease. I don't believe in high-pressure sales. Over the course of the next twenty-five minutes, I want you to look for every reason my product is NOT right for you. I just hope you'll also keep an open mind to determine if it IS something of interest to you. If what I have to share makes sense, I'll ask you to consider taking advantage of it. That's fair, isn't it?" With these words, or something similar, you set the stage. You tell them what to expect. You humanize yourself and make the unknown known. These things relieve pressure. When pressure is relieved, trust has room to grow. You won't regret investing time in creating and using an intent statement of your own.

Another way to develop trust is to tell buyers what you are going to do, then do it. This can be done with something simple during your presentation. For example, "I'm going to take a look at your existing power box so I can speak to your specific situation." Then, you go to the power box, get the information you need, and move on with, "Now that I have seen that, I am able to speak specifically to what you have." This may sound super simple, and it is, but it subtly demonstrates that you do what you say you will. This tends to build confidence in what you say next.

Blending Opposites Takes Practice

Sales can be quite a challenging career until you come to an understanding of its essential elements and how to work with them to your advantage. Many of those elements are complete opposites, and rather than "meeting in the middle," as some might suggest, I prefer to think of it as using those elements to weave or blend together to create positive outcomes. To do so takes us back to my earlier point of working in and on your sales "practice" or, in some cases, "practicing sales."

I like to use the great boxer, Mike Tyson, as an example. How do you think he became great? Did he just decide one day to get into boxing because of his size or build? Did he have the natural aptitude of a great boxer? The answer is no. The reason was that he *decided to become a professional.* He learned how to punch, but he also practiced the opposite, how to block the punches delivered by his opponents. He trained so well and so hard, in the right way, that he no longer needed to think. He developed the reflexes of a world-class boxer.

It's the same for practicing professionals in sales. We must develop our reflexes with the right moves, the right words, and the right actions to earn the respect and trust required for people to want to do business with us. People react to the range of your voice, its volume, pace, and diction, even when they may not understand the words. Your words and actions cause them to think, "Hmm. They look the part and sound the part. They're showing me new information and teaching me something I haven't given much thought to." When they think this, their wariness begins to subside, creating room for trust and respect.

How to Create Opportunities for Decisions to Be Made

In my opinion, well-practiced sales professionals reflexively blend the following:

- Aggressive, yet kind
- Assertive, but nice
- Persistent, but polite
- Pushing and pulling
- Egotistically humble
- Indifferent, yet caring

When you effectively weave these opposite traits or characteristics throughout your communications with buyers, that's when you create opportunities for decisions, otherwise known as "closing."

Aggressive, yet Kind

The type of aggressiveness I'm talking about here has nothing to do with making demands or being confrontational. I'm talking about self-determination. I'm talking about being highly calculated with the strategies you employ. Believe in your product. Believe in its value. Believe in yourself and your abilities to communicate and persuade. Be hard-core on yourself, making forward movement on practicing your skills. You ARE going to make those calls each day. You ARE going to knock on a specific number of doors each day. You attack the day with the high level of determination required to achieve success. Yet, you temper your determination with kindness for yourself and others. When you do this, the combination comes across as confidence, not letting your internal aggressiveness show on the outside with the people you serve.

Assertive, but Nice

Of course, your goal is to complete your job, not just make friends with the people you meet. That's where assertiveness comes in. You have a process to get to that goal. You have developed your questioning and listening skills to control and guide your sales conversations. Yet, you are working with human beings who respond, react, and make decisions with their emotions. You demonstrate respect for their needs, as well as their thoughts and opinions. Yet, you stay on the path toward making sales.

Persistent, but Polite

With persistence, you keep going despite obstacles thrown in your path. Stay focused on the outcome. Do not let those obstacles (also known as objections) undermine your confidence in yourself or your product. Remain polite to those you serve, regardless of the direction the communication takes. Your persistence is rooted in the knowledge that your product serves a valuable need for your buyers. You are confident that owning it is the right solution for the right buyers.

Pushing and Pulling

This is a powerful communication strategy to understand. When you provide information, you are, in essence, pushing others to consider something in a certain light. When you ask effective questions, you are pulling information from others to help you determine their needs. At every stage of the sales process, you must reflexively use the appropriate device to move the sale forward. Is it time to deliver information? Is it time to pause and ask a question? Is it time to reiterate a point? The constant blending of this push/pull motion is what keeps communication flowing and keeps you in control.

Egotistically Humble

Some may say that letting your ego show is a bad thing. I suggest that your ego helps you demonstrate confidence and a sense of pride. Synonyms of the word "egotistical" include self-loving, vain, and proud. You must have a strong sense of self-love to recover from the challenges faced in sales on a daily basis. A level of vanity is necessary to present our best selves. That includes our grooming and dress, as well as how we walk and talk. Finally, being proud of the company and product we represent is absolutely necessary to achieve any level of success.

By blending ego with humility, you prevent pride and confidence from becoming inflated and appearing self-important. Remember, we are working with the mindset of a "servant." We are not concerned solely with ourselves or "taking" advantage of others. Rather, we are focused on "giving" advantages to others through service.

The Impact of Ego Drive and Ego Destruction

To be truly successful in sales, you must be able to sell yourself to yourself. You must know, deep in your mind and heart, that you are helping people to own a product that provides true value for a fair amount. You must be convinced that what you are doing is right and good, and you are a good person for doing so. This means having a strong belief in yourself that comes from within—*ego drive.* It's the motivation you have to achieve your goals and prove yourself.

The key element in benefiting from ego-drive is to keep it internal. Use it to keep yourself going when times get tough, when you face rejection or failure, or when you are disappointed in the results you are seeing. Don't fall into the ego-drive trap of needing external validation for what you are doing, what you believe, and how you plan your life and career. You'll never get that validation from another person. It's more likely that others will question what you are doing, why you believe so strongly in yourself and your product, and wonder about your future. This does nothing but create doubt. So, let's not seek validation elsewhere.

Ego destruction is what happens when you change how you process information about yourself. The simplest explanation is that ego destruction happens when you let what is happening *externally* negatively impact how you feel about yourself *internally*. This is something we all need to learn to control. It's what I am talking about when I say, "I love rejection. Rejection turns me on." I battle ego destruction. I will not allow negative circumstances to change how I think about myself. I remain focused on what I'm doing well or what I am doing right.

If you start reliving or going into a deep analysis of all the things that go wrong in life or in sales, you'll end up pushing yourself into despair. You'll carry that despair into your next sales call, and guess what happens? A downward spiral develops. You struggle to come up with the motivation to make the next call or knock on the next door with confidence. Do this a few times, and it starts to show in your demeanor. People will sense that you don't believe in yourself, or maybe in your product, and they won't want to communicate with you. This leads to frustration.

When most people get frustrated, they either withdraw or become hostile. Neither serves your purpose of achieving success in your sales career. Instead, focus your attention on being creative in each challenging situation. Don't allow the words or actions of others to control your attitude, self-belief, or actions. None of us wants to give control of ourselves to others. It's important to be aware if this begins to happen and take action.

You'll inevitably encounter less-than-stellar situations in sales. You'll be rejected. You'll mess up. You'll inadvertently say the wrong thing to a buyer. It happens. What's important is what you do when it does. If you hang your head, telling yourself things like "This is a bad contact," "They've already been talked to," "They're not interested in my product," all those thoughts and words destroy the ego. They weigh you down. Purposefully focus on your ego drive and beef up your self-talk. Try something like, "I learned so much from that situation. It has made me stronger and better for the next one." This takes practice.

In my door-to-door selling situations, when I leave a home where a door was slammed shut, I tell myself:

"All right! I'm doing well. I'm going to get the next sale, guaranteed. These next people have already been talking about the problem I can solve. They are going to get the product that the last guy refused. The benefit is all theirs!"

By doing this, I'm pushing that last situation out of my awareness and selling myself on the next one before I knock on the door.

The communication you have with yourself is so important. Take a moment to reflect on your own ego-drive and ego-destructive tendencies. Decide how to use them to your advantage.

Indifferent, yet Caring

When you master the blending of these two traits, you'll be on a path to real success in sales. This is when you demonstrate care and concern to gain the benefit of your product but detach from the outcome. If they go ahead, you win. If they don't, you don't lose.

You still care that they are choosing to pass on the benefits. You may set a time to follow up with them, in case they suffer remorse and change their mind. You care enough to remain professional, polite, and kind, and you also have confidence in your performance on their behalf. Don't take their decision personally.

You may never have given this much thought to managing all the aspects of your sales career. It's a lot, and this was only Chapter 3. I encourage you to re-read this chapter once you've completed the rest of the book. It may hit you differently than it does now.

Developing my opposite blending skills, as covered in this chapter, is what made me reflexively flexible and quick to adjust my approach with buyers of different types of products, from various walks of life, and living all over the country. It has allowed me to build a career that supports my goals and dreams.

CHAPTER 4

What It Takes to Be a Highly Skilled Professional Salesperson

AS WITH ANY profession, there are many key elements that contribute to a successful career. It's not just a matter of gaining product knowledge and hitting the bricks to convince others to buy the product you represent. Yes, sales require in-depth product knowledge, but also a high level of communication competence, an understanding of order fulfillment or installation requirements (if your product requires it), a strong self-image, and excellent customer service skills. There are minute details within each component that can make or break your selling days, because sales is both an art and a science.

The science aspect includes the words and phrases covered in Chapter 2, the questions we ask (covered in a later chapter), and the actual steps in the sales process. The art aspect is when and how you apply them.

Some say there are no secrets or shortcuts. I completely disagree. The reason there is so much mediocrity in the field of sales is that people aren't willing to sharpen their skills constantly. They're not willing to seek out or develop secrets and shortcuts to success. They're not willing to become practicing sales professionals. They're not willing to pay the price.

You and I are different. You have chosen to step away from being average by reading this book, being proactive about improving your skills. I continue to dedicate my life to the study of what does and does not work in sales communications, and I am happy to share what I learn. Attention: Everything I teach is based not on theory, but on my actual experiences with more than eighteen years of selling and continued analysis of selling practices.

The Fundamental Ingredients

Throughout my career, I have identified five fundamental ingredients for a successful sales life. I'd like to say that you should fix them in your mind; however, I've heard there's a negative connotation around the word "should." People tend to perceive it as putting pressure on themselves. I get it. If I think I "should" be doing something I don't want to do, I'll probably put it off and feel bad about it at some point in time. Let's rework that concept, like we did with the nasty words in Chapter 2. The only "shoulds" we pay attention to are those we choose, knowing they will truly benefit us.

For now, I'm going to *strongly suggest* you give serious thought and attention to the five fundamentals I'll cover in this chapter. The reason being, I have proven that they make all the difference in my own level of professionalism and the results I've achieved. There's no pressure to do it, but I sure hope you're curious to learn what has contributed so much to my success, and I hope you choose the same.

1. Clarity

Clarity is where the process of becoming a great sales professional begins. I mentioned in Chapter 2 that "a confused mind always says no." That was in reference to our buyers. It's a no-brainer that we want to avoid causing confusion in the minds of our buyers. We need to be very clear about everything we do or say when approaching a potential buyer.

The people we meet are influenced by every aspect of us. They react to our appearance: clothing, stance, and the expression on our face. Their judgment of our trustworthiness begins the moment they lay eyes on us. Nothing visual about us should detract from the level of professionalism we wish to portray. If I could draw you a picture of the ideal salesperson, I would, but they don't exist. Instead, clearly present the best visual version of *you*.

The next area of judgment is what we say: the range, pace, volume, and diction of our voice. Everything must match the perception we want to project. Again, we must be absolutely clear when we speak. Doing so allows buyers to feel that we are transparent with them. This leads to being viewed as trustworthy, honest, and having integrity.

Clarity in your mind is vital. If you are confused, your mind will say no. What does it say no to? Your conviction and belief in yourself, your product, the company you represent, your ability to make sales, and your drive to keep going when the going gets tough—all of it. A lack of clarity will mess with your mind and negatively impact your presentations. It'll be obvious to buyers that you lack clarity and cause them to doubt everything about you.

Having clarity means setting aside any other thoughts and knowing your specific purpose for each communication. My advice is to focus on getting clear, very clear, about your desire to be a true professional, to do what it takes to represent your product properly, and to serve your clients well. Clarity of vision creates conviction; it's essential to your success that you are convinced about what you have chosen to do for a living, so do whatever it takes to do it well.

2. Repetition

It's been proven that it takes a minimum of six repetitions for the human brain to achieve 62 percent retention of new information. This was a huge revelation to me. I figure I'm a smart guy. Once I hear something, I've "got it." That was my ego talking, and that belief was doing me no good. We covered how our ego can cause chaos in the previous chapter and how to master the proper use of it. Remember? Don't let it get in your way like I did early on.

Once I began studying differently: hearing, reading, writing, and saying the words I needed to use *at least six times*, I was able to blend them naturally into my sales process. When my use of those strategies increased, my results improved.

When we learn something new, we possess a certain degree of clumsiness with it. That's normal. Even though we may *understand* a strategy or technique, using it smoothly takes repetitive practice. There's nothing worse than a salesperson who makes it very obvious they're trying to use a technique or strategy on the buyer. It's the best way to increase sales resistance. You cannot be reflexive with an idea, but you can build your reflexes with actual words. When you learn to benefit from the power of repetition, those strategies and techniques become so seamless that buyers don't even recognize them; they just respond more positively.

Understand that the same rule about repetition applies to your buyers. You can't tell them the benefit of your product once and expect them to remember. Build repetition of the most critical points into your presentation. Even better, develop your skills to adapt your presentation to reiterate the points that your buyer reacts to most positively.

This is why I advise you to build your reflexes with your selling skills. It allows you to be flexible. When buyers hear a benefit that appeals to them more than once, it helps build their emotional attachment, ultimately leading to a buying decision.

3. Energy

Salespeople who use their energy most effectively tend to earn the most money. Sure, you might be communicating something to a buyer that you've said a thousand times, but when you match their "first-time" experience with first-time energy, it can be magical. Your level of energy and excitement can impact as much as 51 percent of the sales process.

How to use your energy is one of the most overlooked sales skills. Many of my students experience "aha" moments around this point. Yes, they're aware of their energy throughout each day; they just don't think about proactively employing their energy during sales presentations.

No one wants to hear a monotonous delivery of features and benefits. You can use your energy to dictate your volume, pace, and diction when communicating. When you generate energy and enthusiasm, it becomes contagious to buyers. They feel energized just being around you.

To create energy, I stay highly focused on creating curiosity. I do this by alternating asking questions with sharing information. If someone is not interested in my presentation or product, it's because I'm not interesting enough. Conversely, when I am interesting, my buyers become curious. They ask questions about me, my product, or my industry. When you are excited and you make sense, buyers will be drawn into the process. Curiosity creates involvement.

As a caution, at the beginning of your presentation, you want to match the buyers' energy or be only slightly more energetic. As the presentation moves along, increase your energy, and theirs will likely follow. Practice using your energy at different levels during presentations, and watch what happens. When your energy level is significantly higher than theirs, it can be intimidating. When it's too far below, they're likely to become bored or lose interest.

4. Belief

A common denominator of all top sales professionals is that they shine with what I call "conviction-catching belief" in their product, service, and company. Your belief in the quality and value of your product is critical to your success. Don't take this lightly. Buyers are persuaded more by your depth of conviction than the height of your logic.

If you think you are certain about your belief in your product, ask yourself these questions:

- How strongly do I believe in my product?
- Do I feel good about the benefits buyers receive once they decide to own it?
- Is it a good value?
- Would I purchase it myself?
- Do I believe in the ethics of my company and the quality of service provided after I make the sale?

If you aren't sure, get clear. You will either fall in love with your product and your company, or you may decide it's time to consider representing another product or company.

It's critical to have a deep-down belief about the value of your product or service and your company. If you don't, it'll eventually tear you up inside. It may be evident in your demeanor that you don't truly believe in what you're selling, and your sales will start to decline.

5. Service

When our words and actions are based on a genuine desire to help people, we operate with a servant mentality. When we have taken to heart the previous four fundamentals and recognize our buyers' need for our product, it becomes our obligation to help them own it. In turn, it's our obligation to perfect our skills as assistant buyers to share our knowledge clearly and set the stage, emotionally, for people to make ownership decisions. We automatically focus on the level of service we can provide.

When you align with these five fundamentals, it will begin to feel as though you've fallen into place in your sales career. Your foundation will be strong, and your confidence will grow.

The Personality Traits of Winners

No two days in sales are alike. No two buyers are the same. We have the opportunity to develop our skills and abilities every single day, with every buyer encounter and every conversation with an associate or manager. We can learn something from every communication we have—when we keep ourselves open.

When I analyze various personality traits in myself and other top salespeople who continue to grow, I keep coming back to two that stand out. The two traits I have found necessary to continuously improve are grit and desire.

Grit is also an acronym to me. It is this: "**G**et **R**eady. **I**t's **T**ough." I believe sales is the most challenging career on the planet. Those who can face and overcome the most challenges earn the most money. That's the bottom line of a sales career.

When you have grit, there is no income ceiling in sales. The more courage you have to keep going when things get tough, the better you become. The better you become, the more you will earn.

I view my life as if it were a company stock. I am the company. Everything I do will either put me ahead or behind, make my stock increase or decrease in value. It's my desire to constantly work on increasing the value of my stock. It's my strongest desire. I can only be influenced by outside elements if I allow it. I am the only person who can increase the value of my stock. It is what I focus on at every moment of every day. Whatever I desire, I will work on with grit and determination. I will do whatever it takes to become and remain a highly skilled professional salesperson.

CHAPTER 5

Opposite/Reverse Thinking

DO YOU EVER think about how you think? Becoming a great sales professional starts with how we think. Our thoughts lead to our words. Words create emotions. Those emotions cause us to make judgments. Our judgments lead to our decisions. Decisions determine our wealth. It all starts with the way we think. If you think you were successful in the past, that's great, but understand that the past does not imply success in the future. We have no control over the future. We only have control over ourselves and our reactions to the present moment.

To become more successful in sales, it's important to pay attention to what and how you think. It may come as a surprise to you that most humans are wired with a certain level of negativity bias. We tend to pay more attention to the negative than the positive. The origin of this likely came from our ancient past, when there were more real threats than we have today. That negative bias made us hyper-aware of instances that require our fight, flight, or freeze response for survival. We stayed vigilant, watching for danger at every turn to live another day.

There have been scientific studies that show a higher level of neural processing in the brain when we experience negative versus positive situations. As a result, our behaviors and attitudes are shaped more powerfully by bad news. Negativity bias causes us to dwell on bad thoughts and struggle to keep an optimistic attitude, and that, my friend, is something we must fight daily so we can succeed. We must make conscious efforts to counter that bias and reverse both how we think and act when things don't go the way that we hoped.

It means we must constantly think about what we think about. We have to choose our focus in everyday situations—all day long. Mastering control of our thinking means mastering our resistance to failure, turning rejection into a benefit, and choosing to maintain a positive focus, not letting any negatives slow us down or stop us in our tracks.

There is a great example of this in the use of a reverse poem in a Honda vehicle commercial. A reverse poem uses the exact words and phrases but has a different meaning when read in reverse. Note how the meaning changes at the turning point below, where the words are in **bold**. The poem goes like this:

You won't remember my name.
This is the last time
you will see me at the top.
My doubts
will destroy
my dreams.
The more I seem to learn,
the more I seem to lose.
I want to carry on,
but not today.
This is the point I give up.
But not today.
I want to carry on.
The more I seem to lose,
the more I seem to learn.
My dreams
will destroy
my doubts.
You will see me at the top.

This is the last time
you won't remember my name.

I love this poem and how it's used in this commercial. The point is that belief and resilience will bring you success. I have used this strategy my entire working life. I call it Reverse Thinking.

This is a method of turning every negative situation around to generate positive feelings within yourself to take the next step. If this buyer says no, so what? There's another buyer who will say yes. If I'm going to get rejected, the faster I get to it, the faster I can move on to someone who is interested.

I've worked long and hard on my response to anything negative. It no longer impacts me like it once did. With every negative encounter, I ask myself this question: "Does this situation serve me?" What I'm looking for is whether there is something to be learned. If not, I shake it loose. I've become a "silver lining" thinker, always focusing on how I can create the next positive experience for myself and others.

Sales, for me, is like a video game with me as the main character. I constantly analyze situations and how I will respond. I used to be addicted to video games. Now, I'm addicted to sales, and I am the player.

Motivators versus Demotivators

If you're like me, you have probably had managers or trainers tell you to "stay focused on the positive." That's great advice; however, few go into the detail necessary to do it. This is where a bit of psychology comes in.

You see, we are all either motivated or demotivated when we encounter situations each day. The two greatest motivators are the following:

1. The need to be comfortable.
2. The need to be challenged.

Most challenges get our juices flowing. Simultaneously, everything we do leads us to seek out and accomplish a new level of comfort. However, too much of either comfort or challenge can lead to the two greatest demotivators of all:

1. Burnout
2. Boredom

If we are being challenged so much that we have more anxiety than certainty, we are going to eventually burn out. If we get too comfortable, we are likely to get bored. During some days or "seasons" of our careers, there can be a fine line between the motivators and demotivators.

Too many of us are living in constant conflict between comfort and boredom, challenge and burnout. We strive for the motivators but become paralyzed by the demotivators. The goal is to maintain a creative focus when faced with challenges or create challenges when sensing boredom. That's *opposite* thinking.

I have come across too many salespeople who don't take advantage of opposite/reverse thinking. Instead, they wallow in anxiety and self-doubt. They beat themselves up. They don't consider that others might be intimidated by their potential because they, and only they, are holding themselves back.

I love this quote by Charlie "Tremendous" Jones, and it really applies here: "Growth occurs when you find you can't go on but know you can't quit."

When you feel uncomfortable, choose to think it's because you are facing a growth opportunity. This thought process will alleviate your discomfort and challenge you to think creatively enough to take the next steps toward greater success in both business and life.

Navigating the Swarm of Rejection and Hostility

To keep my focus on the positive, I developed six statements and ideas that serve as reminders to turn my attitude around. I have these phrases ingrained in my brain so I can draw on the strength and creativity I need at any point in time. I highly recommend you do the same.

1. **Flip the Flop**: This is a quick reminder to accept the "flop," the no, and quickly flip my attitude to a positive expectation for the next outcome. This helps me to avoid carrying the negativity of the last "no" into the next sales opportunity. I focus on the next potential "yes" instead.
2. **Quest for the Right Key:** For this one, I use a mental picture of a set of keys on a key ring. If I try one key in a locked door and it doesn't work, I don't toss the whole set, do I? No. I continue to look for the right key. My "keys" are the techniques and strategies I employ with each potential client. By having a variety of "keys," I increase my odds of finding the right one to unlock the barriers, also known as locked doors, that are put in place to deter the average salesperson.

3. **Laugh to Last**: Be amused by hostile people and turned on by rejection. Deciding to be turned on by rejection and laugh, internally, at failure, has made a huge difference in my approach to selling. People who get hostile when I reach out to them are overreacting. They were likely having a bad day before I contacted them. I don't want to contribute to their bad day, and I probably wouldn't want to serve them as clients that day, anyway. When someone says, "I'm not interested" before I get a word out, I laughingly agree with them and say, "Of course, you're not interested. You don't even know why I'm reaching out to you today." This often disarms them. The psychology is to de-escalate their negative emotions and not to let them impact me. They may even realize they're being a bit rude and change their tone. Even if they don't, I've learned to laugh it off as I move on to my next potential buyer. Laughing not only lightens our mood, but it also changes our physiology for the better. Our whole bodies feel better. Laughter is emotional medicine for our souls.

4. **Practice to Ace:** With every rejection or "no sale," I remain firm in my belief that I did my best for that buyer. They have every right to say no, and I

choose to view those as a rehearsal for the next closed transaction. "Practice does not make perfect. Perfect practice makes perfect," as said by the great coach, Vince Lombardi. With every perfect practice, my conviction in myself and my product grows.

5. **Wager to Win**: With every contact, I bet on myself to successfully build rapport. With every presentation, I bet on myself to come away with a closed sale. I am confident in my abilities to help others recognize the value of my product and create feelings within them to want to own it. I may not close every sale, but I will win at keeping my attitude positive and upbeat as I approach the next buyer. I always bet on myself to win!

6. **Pride in Stride:** I am proud of what I do for a living. I take so much pride in helping other people that selling is fun! I enjoy making others proud of me as well: my wife, my dad, my mentor, my training clients, and my business partners. Knowing that I earn their admiration every day keeps my spirits high throughout the day. When I win, they get as much joy from it as I do.

It's the way you think about rejection that matters. When you encounter hostile individuals or struggle to advance a sales process, remember these strategies. Let them help you let go of any stress. I heartily suggest that you read these six ways to practice opposite/reverse thinking often. Use them to begin every day and every buyer encounter with an upbeat enthusiasm and positive expectation.

CHAPTER 6

The Success Triangle for the Practicing Professional

YOU HAVE PROBABLY seen the shape of a triangle used to represent many things. If you do even a little bit of research on them, you'll learn that triangles are hailed by science as the strongest shape. The most basic triangle, which has three sides of equal length, evenly distributes its strength to each side. They are indispensable in engineering and construction.

Many of the wisest people I've studied in the field of personal development also use triangles to demonstrate the equal value of the key lessons they teach. One side is never more important than the other. All three sides combined create a powerful resource.

When considering the key aspects of a career as a practicing sales professional, I developed my success triangle. In my experience, everything we do and say as sales professionals boils down to three key elements of equal importance: technique, attitude, and behavior.

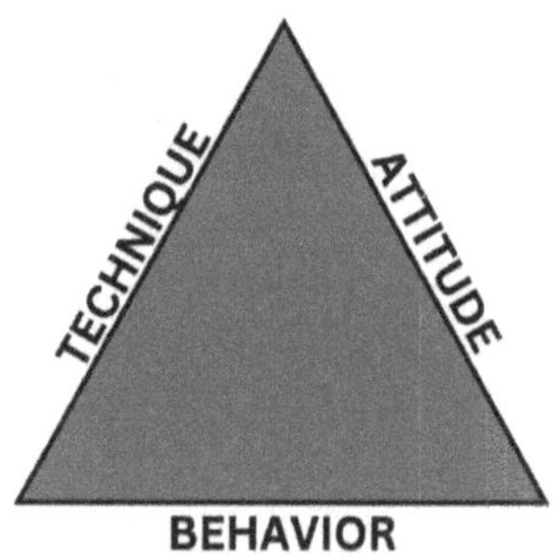

Technique

The first side of the success triangle is your technique. It is how you execute proven methods for engaging with buyers. These are the words that come out of your mouth and how you use your body language to relay information. Sales techniques are the specific communication skills we use.

- It's what you say to connect with people.

- It's the questions you ask to learn about their needs and wants.
- It's what you say as you demonstrate your product with both body language and verbal skills.
- It's how you enhance their belief in you, your company, and your industry.
- And it's how you create strong feelings in buyers, stirring interest in your product that is strong enough to make that final decision to purchase.

Learning proven sales communication techniques is the first step toward becoming a practicing sales professional. As my friend and mentor Tom Hopkins says, "If your tactics are sound, they can't fight you." If you have ever had doubts about "using techniques *on* people," you probably bought into the stereotype, at some point in your life, that salespeople are manipulators. Those stereotypical salespeople probably did "use techniques *on* people." Let me put your mind at ease. Practicing sales professionals don't do that. Instead, the tactics we use *with* buyers are the same ones we use when making decisions for ourselves.

HOW DECISIONS ARE MADE

FOR OURSELVES	HELPING OTHERS
We become educated on the product or service.	We educate them on the product or service.
We consider the pros and cons of owning it.	We explain the pros and cons of owning it.
We weigh our feelings about what the product will do for us.	We say and do things to create feelings in them about the product.
We rationalize our feelings with facts and make the buying decision.	We help them to rationalize their feelings about owning our product and ask for a buying decision.

In sales, we are the guides, the assistants. We help others make decisions the same way we would. In fact, I usually remind the buyers I'm presenting to that "When I'm not working, I'm a consumer, just like you. What I look for when considering any purchase is a quality product, a reputable company, and someone with more knowledge about the product than I have to answer my questions." Most will nod their heads and agree with this statement. And what have I done? I've positioned myself as being "just like them" yet having "more knowledge about the product" to answer their questions.

The techniques of communication and persuasion are the ones we apply to help buyers navigate the decision-making process. Keep in mind that your buyers wouldn't waste their time talking with you if they didn't have at least a fledgling interest in your product or what it can do.

Sales techniques are critical to our success, especially since our focus is on helping people make decisions that solve their problems and enhance their lives. Depending on your product, you may need to help people recognize that there is even a problem to be solved before they'll be curious enough to hear about it. When you are representing something that is unknown to your buyer, you have to use the skills of an educator:

- Capture their attention
- Create curiosity through engagement
- Communicate clearly
- Be adaptable to how they learn and understand
- Have empathy for their situation
- Employ patience while new information is absorbed and processed
- Praise their effort

Like educators, salespeople need to employ the skills of questioning and listening, watching and analyzing. We ask questions and pay attention to how our buyers react to them, as well as listening to how they respond. We watch their body language. We analyze what we did or said and how we might adjust our message to make them feel more relaxed or better about what we are saying. We may even realize they didn't understand us at all and need to repeat the information we shared or provide it differently. This push-and-pull flow of giving information and getting feedback through the use of techniques lets us, in essence, gauge their pulse on how they're feeling at any given moment in the sales process.

Every evaluation we make during the sales process will help us fine-tune our message to the frequency the buyers are on. Sales techniques are the tools we use to do that. We practice them and hone our use of them to succeed at higher and higher levels. All professional performers do this. Watch TikTok and you'll find plenty of people who can do cool dances, but few practice their technique to perform at the level of the highest-earning professionals like J-Lo, Beyoncé, or Bruno Mars. Practice doesn't make perfect, but perfect practice will make perfect.

To do well on this side of the success triangle, understand that there is no natural-born salesperson. You must learn the techniques and strategies that have been proven effective by others in sales. Then, you internalize those techniques so that they come out of your mouth conversationally. If they don't come out naturally, if buyers get the feeling that you are using strategies on them, they'll shut down. They'll stop listening to or trusting what you are saying. So, practice is critical when it comes to techniques. Eventually, you will develop your own style of delivering those techniques, possibly even inventing some new ones of your own.

Early on, the more I learned, the more I knew that I needed to learn. When you start paying attention to the many sales transactions around you daily, your mind may be blown by the smallest thing you see that changes the course of the sales process for the better. There were times when I earned an extra $1,000 from some slight change in technique. That made me hungry to learn even more. Even now, I view techniques as something to help me create my own ATM, spitting out money every time I discover or develop them and then fine-tune them to make them my own.

Attitude

The second side of the triangle is your attitude. This is something that you have to program, program, program, and reprogram constantly. The way you think is the way you are going to achieve. If you believe sales is hard, it will be. If you believe sales is a great career and that you have what it takes to succeed and act upon it, you'll do fine.

You constantly need to sell yourself to yourself. The "you" of today operates on a certain level of programming. The "you" you will become six months or a year from now will likely think differently than you do today. As you grow and become more of a professional, your attitude and self-talk will need to change because you'll be speaking to a better version of yourself.

Learn to work quickly to eliminate the inevitable self-doubt that will creep up on you. When you begin asking, "What am I doing?" "Can I really succeed at this?" "Will I fall on my face?" those are self-doubts. They are perfectly normal reactions to assuming the role of a practicing sales professional. And with sales having a less-than-positive reputation in the world in general, you may have to counter side comments from loved ones about "getting a real job." To counter any negative effect, make yourself pause and reflect on the opposite—writing it out if you must. Here's an example:

- What am I doing? I am actively pursuing success in my career as a professional salesperson. It's an honorable profession, acting as an assistant buyer, helping others make decisions that are truly in their best interest.

- Can I do this? Others have succeeded in this career. I can, too, because I believe in myself and the value of my product. I am willing to do whatever it takes to master proven-effective techniques, so they come across naturally in my conversations with buyers.
- Will I fall on my face? No, because I am surrounding myself with positive energy, constantly observing and analyzing my methods and delivery, and working on perfect practice daily. At the slightest hint of a challenge, I will flex and adapt to present myself and my product well. I have coaches, leaders, and managers in my corner, helping me to improve. I either win or learn with every encounter. Losing is never an option.

Pay attention to what you are saying to yourself throughout the day. Your opinion of yourself is the only one that matters, and once you gain control of any adverse thinking, you will become unstoppable. You will control your attitude so that it only supports your goals and dreams for what a sales career will help you accomplish.

To achieve anything, you must have an absolute certainty of your mission. A common question I hear around goals and plans is this: "What's your why?" Personally, I don't care for it. I think the better question is "Who's your who?" Developing a successful sales practice requires a lot of sacrifices, and the reward of who you're doing it for is a powerful motivator.

- Are you facing daily challenges of selling for your own reward? Are you working to prove yourself to yourself? Like the athletes, are you constantly working on your own personal record, "beating your best" just to prove you can?

OR

- Have you chosen to succeed in sales for what you can do for your loved ones? My dad never had the opportunities I had. I started out doing it all for him—to ease his burden and make him proud. That's what kept me going when I spent all day knocking on doors in 100-plus-degree weather, getting doors slammed in my face, and having people look down on my chosen profession, even going so far as to tell me to get a real job. Does your focus on helping others include sharing the rewards of your efforts with others? If so, recall who uplifts you when you're down and who celebrates your success. Who is your biggest cheerleader? Keeping them in mind will help you keep your attitude on those inevitable tough days.

It doesn't matter which is a bigger motivator for you. What DOES matter is that you recognize what it is that keeps you going. Achieving success in sales may require some temporary imbalance in your life to get what you want, and you *will* do it for yourself or a loved one more than you will for an inanimate goal. People are the reason to make sacrifices, not things, not acquisitions.

Behavior

The third side of the success triangle is your behavior. What you do occasionally will change nothing every single time. What you do daily will create momentum. This is the positive energy and progress that builds over time as you work on consistently improving your behavior as a practicing sales professional. When the momentum is there, you don't even feel like you're working.

When I had 114 roofing sales over eleven days, it felt like I was playing a game. I visualized what I wanted. I verbalized it and acted accordingly. I expected to make those sales. I felt it in every fiber of my being. There was no possible way I was going to act as anything other than a professional assistant buyer to resolve people's problems with their roofs, helping them to get that issue resolved quickly and well.

When it comes to your behavior, beware of the trap of believing that "being busy" every day will create momentum on its own. You probably know someone on your sales team who always appears busy but is not a top salesperson. It's easy to spend all your days on activities that won't lead to sales. It's easy to get side-tracked, too. Don't let that happen to you. Everything you do when you are not presenting or communicating with buyers should be setting you up for when you are.

So, your technique, attitude, and behavior are what contribute most to your professional practice. Evaluate yourself on those three aspects of selling every day. Your strengths and weaknesses will be exposed, and you'll know what to work on next.

CHAPTER 7

The Ps and Ds to Winning as a Sales Professional

TO EFFECTIVELY GET people involved with an idea, a product, or a service requires a process. I mentioned, at the beginning of this book, that I like to keep things simple. I always work on breaking things down to the most basic level. That makes it easier to understand and remember. In this chapter, we'll go over what it takes to win, in the long term, as sales professionals. When you keep these key elements in mind, your sales processes will go more smoothly.

The Ps

I believe there are four key elements to completing an effective sales process: prospecting, presenting, positioning value, and pricing. Sales result when we implement those four elements well.

Prospecting

The best thing I ever heard about prospecting is, "We have to prospect our way out of ever having to prospect." Our goal is to delight the families or companies we serve so they provide us with referrals that generate business for years to come. Having existing clients spread the word about your product and you, as a sales professional, is ideal in this field. Your clients become walking, talking advertisers for you. When satisfied clients recommend you to their friends, relatives, business associates, or even when they give you a testimonial, the first half of your selling process, where you establish rapport and build trust, is pretty much done for you.

Approaching total strangers, also known as "cold prospecting," isn't easy. In fact, it might be the toughest aspect of selling. You'll get a lot more "Nos" than "Yeses" when cold prospecting. It's expected. When you understand and accept this, you can mentally and physically prepare yourself to be patient. It's inevitable that you *will* find someone who is interested in your product or has a need for it. If it's not the person in front of you, it may very well be the next person you meet.

I've thought of myself as "a professional trick or treater" for the last seventeen years as a door-to-door salesperson. Rather than asking for candy, I'm offering to share sweet information about the products I represent. I've reached my highest highs and lowest lows in a twenty-four-hour period while cold prospecting. Throughout that time, I learned a great deal about how to communicate with myself, which is crucial; someone slams a door in my face, and I don't let it get me down.

Initially, I struggled with this. I remember knocking on doors in the heat of a Florida summer when I was twenty years old. I had been dropped off in a neighborhood, and it was my job to knock on every door within a few blocks. After ten hours, I had mostly quick "No, thank yous" and doors slammed in my face, if anyone came to the door at all, and no sales. Feeling defeated, I called my manager. I told him I didn't know what I was doing wrong.

It would have been easy to say that it was a bad neighborhood for our product. It would have been easy to say it was a bad time of day to find people at home. Those are easy excuses in door-to-door selling. Those types of days knock a large percentage of people out of the field altogether. I wasn't ready to give up, but I was hoping for a solution.

My manager asked me how many breaks I had taken. My answer was "None." I hadn't eaten lunch or even sat down to rest the entire time. What my manager said next came as a complete surprise.

"Ten hours and no breaks? That's awesome! That's the best training you can possibly get. This kind of day teaches you a lot about yourself. You are getting so much practice right now," he said.

I had expected some sympathy or even some suggestions about what to do or say at the next door. Instead, he helped me realize that I was demonstrating *my* work ethic. I was strengthening my persistence muscles and learning how to keep myself uplifted. He couldn't do it for me, but he could help me see how I was doing it for myself.

Returning to the "trick or treating" idea, how would you have felt as a kid if your parents just said, "Here, put this mask on, grab a pillowcase, and go knock on the neighbor's doors. When they answer, ask them for candy." Doesn't sound like a good idea, does it? You might even feel weird about it. However, these instructions feel very different and seem reasonable when you know it's Halloween. It's easy to focus on the result of getting candy, and that gets you past the discomfort of doing something "weird." You don't give up when no one is home at the first house, or if you come upon a house where people *are* home but not participating. You don't give up and go home. You keep going. That's the approach I take to prospecting every day that I'm in the field and every day that I'm seeking people to serve with my training business.

I know that my energy and attitude are at their peak after a sale. What I've trained to do is stay in that mindset the entire day, no matter what each door holds. The most important attitude when prospecting is that there is always someone who needs what you have to offer. It's your job to keep going until you find them.

Presenting

Anyone can present. Anyone can show people numbers and follow a sales presentation, document, or system. They can show off a product or a service. The real secret to effective presenting is to present at a certain frequency—the frequency your buyers are on. This is where our tools of observation and analysis come in. We want to match where they are, to speak to them on their level, and educate them to ours. We do this by asking questions to determine their level of understanding of the use and value of our products or services. Once we know that, we can decide where to start with our presentation.

The number one tool in presenting is getting buyers physically involved. If there's a button for them to press, have them do it. If there's something they can hold, hand it to them. With in-home sales, if you can get them to walk with you around their house to show them specific things related to your product, do so. That level of involvement is the most powerful tool in presenting.

People learn through various means, including hearing, reading, writing, and speaking. If you are going to educate them to the point of making a purchase, you need to engage all their senses. You need to build an arsenal of tools to carry with you to every presentation. They'll hear what you have to say. But you also want them to be able to read information that reinforces your verbal message. These may be charts and graphs, specifications, samples, or models. If your product does not lend itself to these visual aids, give each buyer a pen and a pad of paper, and ask them to take notes as you present. This engages them through writing. And with the proper use of questions, you can get them to say what they think and believe about our product. Presenting requires engagement.

Think about how you want someone to communicate new information to you. You are curious to learn but also want the experience to be lighthearted and fun. My goal is to delight the people I serve and help them feel good, even excited, throughout my presentation.

Positioning Value

The ability to position value is the skill most salespeople lack. When value is not properly positioned, buyers will present obstacles or objections to the sale. By positioning value, what I mean is "getting buyers to think differently." When you share new information and they say, "Wow, I never thought about it that way. That does kind of make sense," you have managed to involve them in the sales process.

In the field of solar sales, I often find that people are baffled by what it is and how it works. They can't comprehend its use, much less its value. When this happens, I utilize my general philosophy of breaking things down to their simplest form. I might even slow the pace of my presentation, take a breath, and say, "Ultimately, we are proposing to use your roof as a power plant, no longer being at the mercy of the power company. The sun goes up, and the bills go down." If there is still hesitation, I might lighten the mood by chuckling and saying, "Not sure if you've heard of the sun, but it's pretty reliable and has been around for at least the last few weeks." Many people will smile and realize they have been overthinking their decision simply because solar power is new to them, even if it's not really a new industry anymore.

The idea behind positioning value is to create those "aha" moments, as they cause buyers to open their minds to what you are saying and showing them. The challenge is to incorporate new information, which adjusts their thinking and amends their perspective about their needs and our products as the solution.

Pricing

When you've done the first three steps correctly, the last—pricing—is the simplest. That's because acceptance of pricing always comes down to value. The tipping point for decisions is when people decide that the value of owning our products is greater than the value of keeping their money. It's an emotional decision that they back up with logic.

The key to presenting pricing is to keep your composure—no matter what. You're bound to encounter situations when buyers get super excited about your product, but the price floors them. It'll "cost too much," or they'll want to "think it over" once you come to the point in the sales process for them to make a decision. These are just stalls, and we'll cover how to handle those obstacles in Chapter 13. Even if the buyer loses their composure, you must keep yours. Creating a good opportunity is a state of mind. If you allow yourself to get flustered, you will blow the sales opportunity.

I had the privilege of conducting a training for a company in Canada. The job was to help the field sales team learn how to get people to adopt sustainable energy. They were primarily knocking on doors to find buyers. One of the days I was there, a salesperson set up an appointment with a homeowner to discuss the product. During the initial conversation, the salesperson discovered that the homeowner's energy bill was approximately $50 per month. The engineer at this company informed me that the cost of making the change would be $168 per month on a short-term loan for the equipment.

The salesperson was of the mind that there was no way this person was going to want to triple his bill. I told him that "a good opportunity is a state of mind." When the homeowner came to the door, I opened with, "Thanks for seeing us. I have to tell you that your setup is the best I've seen." I went on to lay out the benefits of his particular property. He became increasingly interested in how he could capitalize on this opportunity for the long term. By the end of my presentation, he was asking me what the next steps were. He went ahead with the purchase, has now paid off the short-term loan, and has long-term equity instead of a liability. This all happened because I didn't let the money get in the way. I knew it was a good opportunity and didn't let the price become a sales killer. When that mindset is at the forefront of your presentation, that energy and enthusiasm will be contagious to buyers.

In some cases, once the pricing is acceptable, we need to close the sale by creating a slight sense of urgency. They've agreed that your product is a reasonable price for the value. The only other question is "when to own it." This can be as simple as asking, "I can arrange delivery on Thursday or next Tuesday, which is better for you?" If they look at their schedule, the sale is confirmed.

The Ds

The six *D*s are: desire, discipline, demonstrate, document, duplicate, and disappear. These six key steps will take you from where you are now to where you want to go. When you understand and internalize these six words, they will quickly help you see your path to success. Once you identify where you are, you'll know which step to take next.

Desire

What do you really expect from your sales career? What do you want it to do for you? Why do you put yourself out there, every day, to face possible rejection? Ask most salespeople and they'll tell you that they do it for the money. I like to go deeper into that question and ask, "What does the *money* do for you?" In most cases, the bottom line is that salespeople view this field as an opportunity to achieve financial freedom.

There's no real income ceiling in sales. As I mentioned earlier, some of the highest-paid "professionals" in the world are in sales. Lots of salespeople's incomes rival those of doctors, lawyers, and CEOs. The top sales professionals earn even more than those professions. One of the main desires is, naturally, income or money and what it will do for them.

For some, it is the general field of competition that drives them. They have a strong desire to win, and sales is an excellent field for that desire. You get to win over the competition. You compete with your fellow sales associates to become the best in your company, or even your industry. Or you compete with yourself to better your previous records. The desire for the challenge of competition is usually strong among top sales professionals.

For others, the strongest desire is to serve. That's me. Yes, I wanted a high income after watching my family barely get by when I was a kid. I do enjoy the challenge of sales. One of the greatest motivators is to be challenged. But I don't compete with other salespeople. I believe that insecurity causes you to compete with others, as though you need to prove something or "one-up" someone. That's not for me. I keep my competitive spirit within. I only compete with the "me" I was yesterday, striving to get better at communicating with customers every day. My strongest desire in sales is to help people live better lives and save money by owning the products I represent.

Think about your desire as it relates to your sales career. Then, ask yourself, "How strong is that desire?" It needs to be very strong for you to do what needs to be done to succeed—to the point of becoming a passion.

Tom Hopkins loves saying, with such force that it's almost a growl, that what we want out of our careers must be "ardently desired." You can feel his intensity vibrate through those words. Do you *ardently* desire to achieve success in sales? If you don't, it's either time to upgrade your skills so you enjoy greater success, or it's time to consider another field. If you have an ardent desire for sales success, you are ready for the next *D.*

Discipline

When you ardently desire success, you will do whatever it takes to develop the discipline within yourself to learn new skills, improve existing ones, carry on when rejected, plan your time and stick to the plan, and go the extra mile. You're never going to be disciplined without an ardent desire for a specific result. And Tom Hopkins taught me that "Desire without discipline leads to disappointment, disillusionment, and depression." Who wants that? No one I've ever met. But discipline is easy when you have the desire.

So, what skills do you need to discipline yourself to learn, practice, internalize, and use? This is where you analyze your weaknesses, make a plan, and set goals to lessen their effect on your results. Please note that goal-*setting* isn't what matters. Yes, it feels good to be thoughtful about what you want to achieve and set goals toward that desire. However, what really matters is goal-*getting,* and that takes discipline.

So, what is it that you need to work on? Do you need to work on time management? Is it your thought process that could use more discipline? Is it how you present yourself, such as your grooming or attire? Is it any aspect of the sales process: your approach, your ability to notice the nuances of others' responses to what you say, the enhancement of your presentation, your understanding and use of questioning, or closing strategies?

Once you determine the area of your life that needs more discipline, write out the necessary actions you must take to change the result you're getting. Then, start acting on it—immediately. You can't think your way to a better life or a more profitable career. You must act. The answers you seek for improvement are found in the actions you avoid.

Another great quote about discipline comes from Jim Rohn, America's favorite business philosopher: "Affirmation without discipline is delusion." Once you understand what needs to be done, don't risk fooling yourself into complacency just because you "understand." Disciplined action is required. You can either take the path of the amateur or the path of the professional. Professionals act. Next, take advantage of the most crucial benefit of being disciplined—consistency. *Consistent discipline* is what makes all the difference when you want more out of your sales career and your life.

Demonstrate

This next *D* is when you practice improved strategies, techniques, and tactics. It is to *demonstrate.*

- Demonstrate your improved mental state with positive internal affirmations.
- Demonstrate your improved physical state with professional appearance and dress, as well as how you carry yourself and act with everyone you encounter.
- Demonstrate the upgraded techniques and strategies you have disciplined yourself to master.
- Demonstrate your product in an improved manner, such that buyers are responding more positively to your offering.

Learning new ways of communicating and new selling strategies is one thing; demonstrating them is something else. It's like the old saying, "Knowledge is power," by Sir Francis Bacon, known for his philosophy of science. We know now that it's not just *having* knowledge that is powerful. The purpose of knowledge is not knowledge, but to create action. It's the *consistent application* of knowledge that makes us powerful. What you do occasionally changes nothing permanently. You can't occasionally do something and expect a long-term result. That is interest, not commitment. Demonstration of what you have disciplined yourself to learn is what makes all the difference in your sales.

With the proper level of discipline, I will go out and demonstrate my skills, my product, and my belief in its benefits on every single sales call. Beyond that, being able to demonstrate how I work with buyers is essential to the development of my training. Time for the next *D*.

Document

How will you verify that the new information you have disciplined yourself to learn and implement is bringing improved results? Well, of course, you'll *know* by your sales figures. But will you know *exactly* what you did or said to yourself or to buyers that worked? You will only know that when you document what you did during every interaction. Document is your next *D* word.

When we document our communications and transactions, we create a valuable resource for both ourselves and those we mentor. We don't allow great thoughts or strategies to get away from us. We want to use them again and again, and having a simple, documented reference will make them readily accessible.

Your documentation can be as simple as a journal (physical or digital) or notes kept in your phone. What's important is that you exercise that earlier *D*—*discipline*—to document everything. What are you going to document? Here are a few questions to get you started:

- What were you thinking before that last positive transaction?
- What were you thinking before the last transaction that didn't result in a sale?
- How did you present yourself to buyers who made purchases?
- What did you observe in the buyers' environment? Did you use those observations to help them like you or build trust?
- What did you say to build rapport?
- How was it, exactly, that your presentation went?
- Were there interruptions by the buyers? If so, how did you handle them?
- How did you stay on track in the sales process?
- What closing strategy or strategies did you use, and how effective were they?

This may seem like a lot, but when you start making notes consistently, you will see patterns emerge. You'll see the proof that what you have disciplined yourself to master is working. It's proof of how impressive your skills are and how well-perceived your product is.

Your documentation will show the story of your success. Your story will impress others and make them want to do what you are doing. No one wants to be recruited or managed without knowing that you have had greater success than they have. They want to know your story. They want to be impressed enough to follow your lead or take your advice. Your documentation provides the proof. This leads us to the next *D*.

Duplicate

Once you have documented the details of your transactions, it will become easier to duplicate your efforts. As you use your successful strategies repeatedly, they will become even more ingrained and unconsciously practiced. Once they come to you naturally, you will likely build upon that foundation by tweaking what you say and do for even greater results.

When you can prove that you can duplicate your results, others will be drawn to you. Your documentation will tell your story and show others how to succeed as you do. It's what you use to break down your steps to success and teach others to do the same. The secret to living is giving. The more you can share with others, the better. If you and I can teach others how to improve their careers and their lives, that's the most satisfying reward ever. Some may not have the same opportunities you and I have, but when we can show them how to have more of the success they desire, it gives life purpose.

Duplication is also important because it's what needs to happen for you to move up or on in your career. Through duplication, you can take advantage of the next *D*.

Disappear

Through duplication, you can disappear. What I mean is that you can work yourself beyond your current position or level. You can move from being a salesperson to becoming a leader, a regional representative, a vice president, and so on, up the chain. The authority of moving up allows you to influence others and become an inspiration. You get to experience new levels of comfort in your life, but challenge yourself even more. For me, after achieving each new level of success, I ask myself, "How far can I go? What does the view from here show me that I couldn't see before?"

Another aspect of disappearing is that you might even be able to stop working altogether. The typical salesperson I meet tells me that earning $100,000 is a successful year. Those people might be happy remaining at that skill level and continuing to earn around that same amount each year, but they don't get to disappear. It's discipline and sacrifice that allow you to disappear. My top student so far earned over two million dollars in a single year. He created the option to hang out on a beach somewhere, no longer working for the next twenty years.

As a quick recap, here's what the six *D*s will do for you: Your *desire* will encourage *discipline.* The discipline will allow you to *demonstrate* improved skills. The *demonstration* will give you something to *document.* That *documentation* will allow you to *duplicate* your success, and the *duplication* will enable you to *disappear.* Now comes the biggest question of all.

Are You Willing to Pay the Price?

In my experience, the biggest difference between practicing sales professionals and average salespeople is a lack of willingness to pay the price to succeed. It takes a concerted effort to follow the formula of the six *D*s. It takes time to practice enough to get it right. It takes dedicated sacrifice. If you're not currently operating at your peak, you will need to make some changes to get where you want to go. In my experience, the words "success" and "sacrifice" go hand in hand.

What are you willing to give up in exchange for a higher level of satisfaction and success? Remember those other practicing professionals? Doctors and athletes are willing to pay the price required to achieve. Their paths are not easy. Nothing truly worthwhile is easy. However, when the path is laid out clearly for them and the advantages of taking it make sense, they do what it takes to get there.

Do you genuinely want to earn a potentially equivalent income to that of the top sales professionals and enjoy the job satisfaction of helping others? Do you have the willingness to pay the price? The price of effort, learning, time, and dedicated sacrifice. The other option is going to a place called Someday Aisle. Someday, I will commit to the hours. I will be great. I will be a professional. It's just south of Procrastination County.

CHAPTER 8

The ABCs of Selling

PRACTICING SALES PROFESSIONALS are constantly seeking better ways to communicate with buyers. They understand that everything they do and say needs to benefit them and their buyers. Everything must accumulate into one emotional decision to make the purchase.

How do we do that? It's as simple as learning your ABCs. You may have heard that the ABCs of Closing stands for "Always Be Closing," and that is true. You are working toward the close with every word and every action, down to the smallest details, including how you handle your presentation materials and even the pen used for signing the buyer.

However, before we make strides with the ABCs of Closing, I believe we should have a solid understanding of the ABCs of Selling. These are the fundamentals that will lead you to a more successful career.

A is for Attitude

Attitude is how you internalize failure and rejection. As I mentioned previously, rejection turns me on. I love hostile people. Encountering them is inevitable. Rather than avoiding them or letting their anger get to me, I use their hostility as gasoline for my tank. I let it amuse me and spur me on.

Choose to think about that inevitable failure and rejection as a motivator. Don't let it get to you. I was passing by a church one day while selling alarm systems in Flint, Michigan. The church had a sign outside with the statement, "He who angers you controls you." That stuck with me. When someone gets upset with me or rejects what I'm offering, I just say, "Thank you," and move on. None of us wants to let others control our feelings. We control them. The secret is to have fun. If you're not having fun in sales, it's not worth it. Maintaining something that's not fun will eventually become exhausting. Building something that is fun is energizing.

The secret ingredient is that the way we think will change the direction we move in. Are you starting sales calls with confidence or uncertainty? You get to choose. Certainty comes from practice—be a practicing sales professional.

B is for Balance

Being in balance means having total fulfillment in all areas: financial, emotional, physical, and spiritual. An occasional or temporary imbalance may be necessary to achieve your career goals. The ultimate life goal is to strive for balance in all areas. Take a moment to reflect on your goals and make a plan.

What's important to you? What are your core values? Your values make you do the things that are not easy. You don't want to live life based on somebody else's values. Examples: Flexibility, Family, Adventure, Health, Financial Freedom, Impact, Influence, etc.

1.____

____

____

____

2.____

____

____

____

3.____

____

____

____

4.____

____

____

____

5.____

____

____

____

What are your “BIG 5” for the year? (Top five goals within the next twelve months)

1.____

2.____

3.____

4.____

5.____

What are your top three goals for the next ninety days? (Must be parallel with yearly goals)

1.____

____

____

____

2.____

____

____

____

3.____

____

____

____

Top Three Focuses for Month One:

1.____

____

2.____

____

3.____

____

Top Three Focuses for Month Two:

1.____

____

2.____

____

3.____

____

Top Three Focuses for Month Three:

1.____

____

2.____

____

3.____

____

What are your three most compelling reasons to hit those goals and elevate your life?

1.____

____

____

____

2.____

____

____

____

3.____

____

____

____

C is for Confidence

Act it, and you become it. First comes the action, then comes the motivation. First, you move, then you have the power. Visualize what you want to accomplish, verbalize it, then take the first steps. Your confidence will strengthen with each step forward.

Brainstorm the steps you can take to achieve your goals from the previous section with confidence:

D is for Discipline

As Tom Hopkins told us, "Desire without discipline leads to disappointment, disillusionment, and depression." Discipline is one of the most essential character traits to develop.

Where do you lack discipline, and what could you do to improve in this area to the benefit of your goals?

E is for Enthusiasm

Enthusiasm is the spirit that resides within you. Your level of enthusiasm, in my experience, impacts as much as 51 percent of the sales process. If you're not excited about your product, your service, and your life, people will read right through you. If you aren't enthusiastic, you can't expect others to become enthusiastic about your product or presentation. Even if it's the twentieth time you've given your presentation this week, deliver it with a fresh, first-time level of enthusiasm. After all, it's the first time your buyer has heard it.

The word enthusiasm is derived from both Latin and Greek. Both meanings include the word "inspiration." How does it feel when you are inspired by something? Maybe even passionate? You feel something profound that energizes you with enthusiasm for life, family, career, and each connection with buyers.

Tom Hopkins suggests that the ending of the word enthus*iasm* should remind us of the acronym, "I Am Sold Myself." Facing each sales day with enthusiasm lets us demonstrate how sold we are on our product, field of work, and ourselves. Enthusiasm is a vital part of the foundation of a successful sales career, as well as a happy and satisfied life.

F is for Flexible

Anything is feasible if you are always flexible. If you have been in sales longer than a few months, you know that sales professionals can have the highest highs and the lowest lows within a twenty-four-hour period. That rollercoaster ride, for most of us, is part of what we love about this business. It's a daily challenge.

We must remain flexible in all things because we can rarely control the entire flow of our days. We might randomly encounter a buyer who needs an immediate solution. We may have one or more "visits" canceled at the last minute. We must train ourselves to be prepared to pivot our daily plans on a moment's notice. Develop your flexibility. Learn to bend, and you won't break. Always have something else to do that will propel you forward if and when the timing of your day changes.

What are some ways you could pivot when your day is thrown off course? What is your backup plan?

____

____

____

____

____

G is for Goals

Set goals for everything. There are two main types of goals: short-term and long-term. Long-term goals are for the life you want to live. Short-term goals can include making a certain number of calls each day or obtaining the desired response from a single contact.

All of your goals must be better than your current best, but believable. Long-term goals must be worth committing to—and they must be yours. Don't set long-term goals to live the life of someone else. You are a unique individual. Invest a lot of time and thought in determining what long-term goals are worth working toward for the next twenty years or more.

Short-term goals can be for a moment, a day, a week, or a month. I don't advise setting short-term goals for more than ninety days. Anything over ninety days should be considered a long-term, or lofty, goal.

The energy and focus required to achieve lofty goals can be quite a strain. For your loftiest goals, break them down into smaller, manageable parts that are challenging yet feasible to accomplish.

Tom Hopkins taught me that most people spend more time planning the details of a two-week vacation than they do thinking about how they want to live, even five years from now, much less investing time in planning the details for their lifetime accomplishments. If you don't know where you're going, how will you know how to get there? Commit to choosing who you want to be, how you want to live, and what you want to do twenty years from now. Block the time in your schedule to think about this and plan for it within the next week. Make it non-negotiable. Decide what will truly inspire you to accomplish your goals. Then, share it with your closest loved ones because that's who you'll want to celebrate with.

H is for Health

This should be very obvious. Getting rich and sick is stupid. To have the energy we need to accomplish the goals we ardently desire requires having a healthy body. Developing commitment and discipline to take care of our bodies is critical.

When I realized that I had let my health slip due to my travel schedule, I knew I had to act. I can't expect others to do what I suggest if I'm not doing it. Once I admitted to myself that I had a problem, I committed to swimming one hundred laps in a pool every day for one hundred days. That goal was challenging but achievable to me. Swimming is great exercise. You're unlikely to pull a muscle or damage your joints while doing it, and it's great for your cardio. Pools are pretty much accessible anywhere I travel. So, I figured out how to add "swim time" to every day on my schedule.

Even on days when I had a full schedule, I switched things around to make this happen. Then, I posted my goal on my social media account. I asked people to state in the comments how long they thought I would make it. I offered to pay the winner $1,000. One person posted that they bet I'd make it ninety-nine days. I didn't want to pay out the thousand, so that became an added motivator for me to meet my goal. I made a game out of it. I was excited to hit the pool every day and prove that guy wrong.

And you know what? I didn't quite make it. On day seventy-nine, I tore my anterior cruciate ligament (ACL) playing basketball. Even though I was struggling to walk, I continued to swim for three more days, determined to reach one hundred. On day eighty-three, I had to admit that continuing to push myself in the pool was no longer in the best interest of my health. So, I stopped. Rather than viewing the situation as a failure to meet my goal, I kept in mind how much regular swimming had improved my overall physical health. Even better, I recognized that the discipline of swimming every day gave me a huge mental health boost.

I is for Integrity

Be trustworthy so people will want to do business with you. The number one rule of ethics in selling is this: If someone qualifies by means of wants, needs, and financial capability to own your product or service, you must sell them, get them involved, or help them acquire it. It becomes your obligation to educate them, so they see it as a no-brainer, and they are happy to make the decision to move forward. Now, if somebody does not qualify due to needs, wants, or financial capabilities, we must guide them to whatever decision serves them.

J is for Just for Today

Live in the present. Burn the past. Today is all we have. There's no need to dwell on anything that happened yesterday or any day before. When the average person gets frustrated, they tend to dwell on what hasn't happened, rather than what is happening right now. They are more likely to get depressed, withdraw, become hostile, or even quit. When frustration raises its ugly head, winners ask themselves, "How can I be creative in this situation?"

Frustration combined with creativity will allow you to stay focused on the situation in the moment and make it better.

What present situation do you need to approach with more creativity? Use this space to brainstorm creative approaches:

____

____

____

____

____

K is for Knowledge

Knowledge is power when it is appropriately applied. If you learn all the strategies in this book or from any source, and you believe you "know," I'll tell you now that you don't really "know" anything unless you apply that "knowledge" to making your life or the lives of your buyers, or even your loved ones, better. Strive not only to gain knowledge, but to apply it as soon as possible.

L is for Laughter

Who doesn't enjoy laughing? Even in the Bible, it is written in Proverbs 17:22 (NKJV) that "a merry heart does good, like medicine, but a broken spirit dries the bones." Seeking something to be light-hearted or even heartily laugh about is another way to take care of ourselves, both mentally and physically.

There was a top sales consultant back in the 1960s named Elmer Wheeler. He coined the famous phrase, "Don't sell the steak—sell the sizzle." He was right. But, more importantly, Mr. Wheeler taught an excellent strategy to help sales professionals avoid employing a fake smile or forced laughter with buyers. Take a moment, right now, to close your eyes and picture a five-month-old baby. Imagine how innocent and happy they are. Then, open your eyes and smile, chuckle, or laugh like you would if you were engaging with that infant. Your smile will be sincere from your chin to your eyes. That's Mr. Wheeler's "Smile Formula" to practice when engaging with others. Not only will your smile be genuine, but you will also feel a deep sense of enjoyment within.

M is for Mentor

Allow yourself to be mentored and commit time to mentoring others. There are three specific individuals to identify, along these lines, for career success. The first person to identify is someone you want to emulate. It's someone who is being, doing, or having what you want in your life. It's the person you want to be like. The second person is your competition. Initially, you may think the biggest competitor is someone with more sales or who makes more money. However, after listening to the audiobook *Outwitting the Devil* by Napoleon Hill, I realized my biggest competitor was the devil trying to get me off track, trying to prevent me from being the best version of myself. Remember, whatever is in your awareness is within your control. The third person you want to identify is someone who could benefit from what you've already become or accomplished. This is someone you might mentor or may already be mentoring, even if your relationship is not defined as such.

Have you ever helped or tried to help someone else with something you have already done or know how to do in sales? If so, how did it make you feel? Did you sit up a little straighter? Did you put extra effort into demonstrating your skill exceptionally well? I would suggest that you give more thought to your performance when helping another person learn. Mentoring, whether receiving or giving, is fundamental to becoming a better version of yourself.

N is for Network

With every person you meet, you expand your potential client base. Your network is your net worth. For me, currency is no longer just money; it's the quality of the relationships I have. How do you want to be remembered?

____

____

____

____

____

O is for Organized

When you are organized, it becomes easier to pay attention to the details of your relationships and keep track of your clients' needs. You will also be able to focus more on how you present yourself to the world and what you do and say daily. When you are not organized, you waste a significant amount of valuable time searching for things or information. Being well-organized is a great way to create a positive impression with others, and it lends itself to building trust.

In what ways could you improve your organization on a daily basis?

____

____

____

____

____

P is for Persistence

The most important application of persistence needs to be within yourself. You can be a bulldog going after business, but when you are persistent in developing your personal growth, that's when everything gets better. Be firm with yourself. Make it a habit to tell yourself "One more" when you are tempted to stop:

- One more time practicing my presentation
- One more questioning strategy to master
- One more close to memorize and rehearse
- One more call to make
- One more message to send to stay connected with clients

Make "one more" your mantra. When you develop your "one more" staying power, you will consistently outperform the competition.

Q is for Questions

I am like a police officer in selling situations: "Anything you say can be held against you." I ask a lot of questions and write down the answers people provide. I use their own words to take them through the sales process. "You mentioned ___ is your biggest challenge. Here's what this product will do to fix that." When buyers tell us their biggest challenge, and our product can resolve that, we're more than halfway to a closed sale.

R is for Relationships

Beginning with rapport, develop respect and give the people you serve more than they expect. When you stay in touch and frequently communicate, your past clients will provide more business, either directly or by referring others.

S is for Success

Tom Hopkins defines success as a continuous journey toward achieving predetermined, worthwhile goals. It's not a landing place. It's a journey. And most importantly, it's a journey you choose to take because it means something to you. With this definition, success is something you can experience every moment of every day. It's something you "become" a little more each day.

T is for Time Planning

We must do the most productive thing possible at every given moment. The only way to be truly productive is to plan your time. When you hold yourself accountable for investing your time wisely, you can eliminate those unproductive, time-wasting habits from your life.

Time planning can create greater satisfaction in general. If you find yourself with time slots that you're not sure what to do with, use that time to learn something new. Doing so is never a waste of time.

U is for Understanding

We don't meet with buyers to be understood. We make time to visit with them to better understand their needs, wants, desires, and problems. People don't buy from you because they understand what you're saying. They buy because they feel understood.

V is for Vocabulary

The words we use fuel thoughts and feelings that result in actions. How well are your words serving you right now? If you're not achieving the level of success you desire, it may be time to up your game with your vocabulary. Review the nasty words and their replacements covered in Chapter 2. Have you incorporated all of them into your presentations or your daily conversations? If not, work on that.

If you have already begun using them naturally, review your presentation and look for places where you might insert some glamour words. Consider your explanation of the product from the buyer's viewpoint. Are you using industry jargon that they might not fully understand? How can you simplify your explanation of the product? If your typical buyers are primarily from a specific field, such as the medical field or construction, have you incorporated some of their industry-specific terminology into your presentations? Can you draw analogies between your product and their services?

As an example, let's say your clients are mostly architects. Have you read the latest news about their industry? It might be wise to do so or even subscribe to their industry publications. Not all of the information will be valuable, but using even a bit of their vocabulary will go a long way toward building rapport and trust.

W is for Work

Life works when you work. What is your perspective on work? Do you see it as something you "have to" do? When you love what you do for a living, it's not work. When you choose to view what you do for a living as performing a high level of service to others, it's not work. And when you do it well, things work out well for you.

Take a moment to reflect on what you love about your work and how it serves others:

____

____

____

X is for Extra

Find creative ways to give thanks and recognition to your company's clients. Always give information, advice, and service. Always give more than people expect. Going the extra mile with and for others always reaps its reward. Sometimes, I leave a handwritten thank-you note, bring a small gift, or order something on Amazon.

Y is for Why Wait?

Remember when we covered procrastination? Waiting ruins your future. It causes you to avoid the present because you live in the past. When you prioritize doing the most productive thing (see time planning), you can train yourself to focus on what is most important. Do it now. Don't wait. Don't allow anything to weigh on you or hold you back on your journey to success.

Z is for Zeal

To reinforce your memory of this one, I'm asking you to *zero in with zeal*. By this, I mean to focus on what's important, maintain a positive frame of mind, and utilize your energy and enthusiasm to improve every day. A salesperson is most contagious right after they get a sale. After many slammed doors in my face, I kept saying to myself, "That was great! I'm on fire today!" It kept my momentum going so I could be ready for the next client.

Reread this chapter every day for a while. The messages will become ingrained in your psyche. Get to where you can recite the word for each letter as well as recite the ABCs themselves. These reminders will become natural contributors to your well-being and success.

CHAPTER 9

The Most Powerful Technique in All of Selling

EVERY INTERACTION WITH buyers can take many different directions. Practicing sales professionals don't worry about this because they understand the most powerful technique of selling and master it. This technique is called "taking the command position." It allows you to get and maintain control of every interaction. When you lose control of the conversation, you lose the sale—every time.

When you take the command position, you are in charge of the sales process. You orchestrate every aspect.

You direct the ebb and flow of communication. Even when you ask questions to allow the buyer to provide information, you direct the conversation.

Please understand that this is not manipulation. It's keeping the sales process, the sales process. It's a method of staying on task. Sure, you want to enjoy getting to know your buyers, but you are not speaking with them to make new friends. Your time with them has a purpose, and it's up to you to ensure that it's accomplished. You are setting the tone and pace of the process at all times.

If a comment or sidebar takes you off course, bring the conversation back on track with follow-up questions. Reconnect with their curiosity about your product's features and benefits. All techniques and strategies, when used properly, are control devices that allow you to command the attention of the buyer and build their emotional interest to make an ownership decision.

You, the expert on your product or service, must take the command position. Would a five-year-old reach out to take the hand of an adult to walk that person across the street? No, because they don't have the knowledge or skill to take control of such a situation. It would be the opposite—the adult taking the hand of the child. As the assistant buyer, it's your job to take the command position and assist or guide the buyer to a deeper understanding of the problem/solution aspect of your product by asking questions. Knowing what you know, you've already decided what is best for the buyer. You're just asking a lot of questions throughout the sales process to confirm it, for both of you, before asking for the sale.

If you allow the buyer to take the command position, it's highly unlikely you will close the sale. An example of this is responding to their request for the price before you've even determined if they're qualified or explained your product and built value.

To maintain control of the sales process in this situation, you would say something like this: "Ms. Parker, the amount people invest in this type of product can vary considerably. I wouldn't want to suggest anything that's not in your best interest. So, with your permission, let's determine if my product is even the right solution for you before discussing price." Then, ask a question that takes you right back into the step of the sales process where you were heading before her request. The phrase, "in your best interest," here is what you want to emphasize. It reinforces your position as an assistant buyer rather than as an adversary.

Taking the Command Position

There are a few principles to consider when taking the command position. First, it's essential to establish rapport before attempting to direct the narrative. How much time this takes will vary, but keep in mind that you'll stack the odds against yourself if you do it too quickly. Once you sense the buyers are open to at least hearing a little about what you're offering, that's the time to take control using your questioning strategies.

The next principle is that you can't lead people to decisions unless or until you make them first. Envision the options of your product or service like a flow chart. You ask the questions. If the answer is A, you follow that line of questioning to determine if that product is right for them. If the answer is B, follow that one. Along each line of questioning, any answer the buyer provides could shift the direction you need to take next. This is where your preparation as a practicing sales professional comes in. You are the expert. You know your product so well, and they don't. It's your job, duty, and obligation to guide them to the ONE solution that will best suit their needs. And with the command position, you're doing it effectively and efficiently, not wasting their time or yours.

Another option to consider is to move along with your questions. As soon as they answer one question, acknowledge it and ask another. You are prepared to flow through the sales process; don't allow time for them to interrupt with sidebars or go off on tangents. If they give you an answer you didn't expect, you may have to make a slight course correction, but this is where the preparation of your reflexes comes into play. Flex quickly to get back on course or cover any point they deem distracting.

Keeping Control with Questions

The best demonstration of how to use questions to guide others is what Tom Hopkins calls his "card trick analogy." He would demonstrate this during his seminars by asking someone in the audience to help him.

What happens when people say, "You wouldn't mind helping me for a moment, would you?" or "I need a little help"? Most people lean in or come closer to determine if they can help. Most members of the human race are kind at heart. If they believe they can do something simple or quick that will help another, they'll do it. I use a variation of those sentences to engage nearly every homeowner during field training for my door-to-door clients. For example, I might make small conversation by asking them for directions or whether or not they are familiar with the area.

With Tom's card trick, he has another audience member choose a card from a deck and show it to the audience. The volunteer does not see it. Tom then asks a series of questions that the volunteer can answer in one of two or three ways. Each of their answers leads to the next question, and so on, until their final answer is precisely what Tom wants them to say, the name of the card that was chosen. The point of the exercise is that, with proper questioning, assistant buyers can guide buyers to their own conclusions about products—conclusions that match what the assistant wants to happen, which is the buyer choosing to make the buying decision.

If the card drawn is the jack of clubs, the questioning sequence would sound something like this:

> Tom: "You've played cards once or twice, haven't you?"
>
> Volunteer: "Yes."
>
> Tom: "Great. Then you are aware that there are fifty-two cards in the deck, isn't that right?"
>
> Volunteer: "Yes."
>
> Tom: "Now, those fifty-two cards are broken into two colors, aren't they, red and black?"

Volunteer: "Yes."

Tom: "Would you name either the red or the black?"

Volunteer: "Red."

Tom: "All right, and that would leave you then with the black, wouldn't it?"

Volunteer: "Yes."

Tom: "Now, with the black cards in the deck, there are spades and clubs. Would you please name either the spades or clubs?"

Volunteer: "Clubs."

Tom: "That's right. Now, in the set of clubs, there are face cards and number cards. Please name either face or number."

Volunteer: "Face."

Tom: "That's right. Now, in the face cards, we have three choices: the jack, king, or queen of clubs. Would you name the jack, king, or queen of clubs?"

Volunteer: "Queen."

Tom: "And that would leave you with the king or jack. Would you name either the king or the jack of clubs?"

Volunteer: "Jack."

> Tom: "I think you found it. It sounds like you've decided on the jack of clubs, is that right?"
>
> Volunteer: "Yes."

This is a fun exercise to do with friends or kids. They follow right along and are often amazed that they guess the correct answer. Doing so allows you to practice getting comfortable with guiding questions, whether you receive the answers you expect or not.

This strategy involves always asking your buyers questions that you know they can answer. Start with general questions, then gradually get more specific. When their answer is going in the direction you want, agree with them. When it's not, redirect the conversation with another question.

The real benefit comes when you apply it to your product or service. Do you see how you could use questions to control the conversations in which you guide your buyers toward choosing to own your product? The key (to everything in life) is to ask the right questions to lead or guide people to a decision you have already made.

The Pattern Interrupt Strategy for Regaining the Command Position

When you feel the buyer's wall of resistance building or a negative trend in their responses, use a technique called "the pattern interrupt strategy." It's where you ask a question that is not related to the sales process. It interrupts both the direction of the conversation and allows you to reset the buyer's feelings about you and the conversation. It's designed to interrupt the negative direction of the sales process *and* turn their attention to something they feel positive about. The interruption alters the anticipated flow of conversation and prompts an automatic shift in perspective.

It can also be used to plant the seeds of a "Yes" momentum. Through the proper use of questioning strategies (as I cover in Chapter 10), you regain control of the conversation and steer it back to building their curiosity and getting their approval to move forward in the sales process.

If you realize the buyer's *emotions* about the sales process are taking a negative turn, it's time to steer them in a different direction. I know I said people buy emotionally and rationalize logically, but when their emotions are trending negatively, we need to change their focus. A switch to the rational perspective is a great use of the pattern interrupt strategy. It might sound like this:

"Sir, we can take all the emotion out of this conversation and see if this is a logical decision for you to go ahead. If it is, you'd probably want to take care of it and move on with your day, wouldn't you?"

With those words, you're demonstrating that you don't want to waste their time, which most people will respect. This can help quickly diffuse their negative emotions and allow you to regain control of the sales process with a recap of the logic behind the value of your product.

This is a scenario where I might stop mid-sentence and ask, "Jim, may I have your permission to be blunt?" Most buyers are taken aback by this question. If they don't respond positively right away, I just continue like this:

"I've done this for so long. Typically, when people get into this situation, deep down, they know what they really want. But what happens is people tend to make this a much bigger decision than it really is, and they end up doing nothing. If everything that I have laid out for you today is accurate, do you think you'd lean more toward going ahead or not going ahead?"

Those words diminish the effect of their emotions and increase their desire to rationalize the decision. At this point, the decision becomes more "black and white" than colored by emotion.

If their answer is "not going ahead," I use a strategy called the "Take Away" (covered in detail in Chapter 11) and start packing up any materials I have used. The take away often makes them reconsider due to a natural fear of scarcity we all have. It doesn't work every time, but it does allow you to leave the opportunity with a good conscience.

Am I still in command when this happens? Yes, 100 percent. I might continue by saying, "I don't believe in high-pressure sales and wouldn't want you to regret the purchase." Assistant buyers never want to push people into making decisions. Instead, the goal is to pull them toward the realization that their lives or businesses will be better off by owning the product.

Remain in command of the conversation even when it doesn't end with a sale. This sense of power will guide you to the next potential buyer with a positive mindset.

CHAPTER 10

Questions Are the Answers

QUESTIONING AND LISTENING are two of your most valuable communication skills. There won't be much to hear unless you get really good at asking the right questions. Practicing sales professionals know that the only thing more important than learning the ins and outs of their product is how to ask effective questions that engage and retain buyers. Questioning skills are something *every* sales professional needs to master.

I'm often surprised to learn how many people who call themselves sales professionals do not understand the incredible power of asking the right questions. They believe that asking questions is so fundamental that they don't properly consider their use as sales tools.

Tom Hopkins shared a story with me about a major international company that hired his team to teach a small, yet top-notch sales team in one of their regions. It was the regional director's idea to reward this team with an opportunity to do even better. The internal corporate training department was strongly opposed, as they believed their in-house training was sufficient.

When the training was over and the evaluations reviewed, the most appreciated strategies were on the subject of asking questions. The corporate trainers were shocked. Their response was "Everyone on the sales team has a college degree. They should all know how to ask questions." The misconception was that basic communication skills and sales communication skills are the same. Although both types of communication may employ the same types of questions, for sales, there are also specific "questioning *strategies*" to use. It's the strategies that make all the difference in the results you get.

Practicing sales professionals will listen twice as much as they talk. Tom Hopkins taught me that when you're talking, you can only cover what you already know. When you ask questions to get others talking, you learn something new. With the right questions, that new knowledge helps you move the sales process forward. When questioning strategies are correctly applied, you will learn the following:

- What your buyers already know about your product, if anything. This will help you determine where to start educating them about its features and benefits. Your approach will be very different if you're representing a type of product they've never heard of versus a new and improved version of something they're familiar with.
- How your buyers feel about your product. This will help you determine whether you need to build their confidence in the product as a whole or just in *your* brand. Note: You may learn that their sales resistance is due to a bad experience, and you'll have to hear them out about that before moving forward.
- What their needs are. Once you understand how they view the problem your product resolves, you'll know which offer to present and what hot buttons to push when discussing the product or service.

- What their wants are. If you sell something to replace what the buyer already has, you'll ask questions to learn about their ideal solution. You will learn whether they would be happy with something equivalent or if they are seeking something better. If you have a better product, service, or program, you may want to present a more enhanced solution than initially planned.
- Who will make the final decision? Sure, you may be speaking with someone who has put themselves forth as the decision-maker, but when it comes to actually spending money, another party may need to be consulted or even approve the paperwork.

With the right questions asked at the right time, you are in absolute control of the sales conversation and can keep the sales process moving forward.

Why We Ask Questions

There are several reasons why practicing professionals ask questions differently from average salespeople, including why they strategically ask sales-specific questions. The main reason is that people don't always believe what we say. However, they do believe what *they* say. Another Hopkins quote is "When I say it, they doubt it.

When they say it, it's true." Getting them to say what they believe is what makes sales questioning strategies powerful.

Here are some of the other reasons why we ask questions strategically:

- **Take the Command Position.** The person asking the questions has control over the direction of the conversation.
- **Isolate Areas of Interest.** Use questions to guide buyers down a path of this or that. Utilize the answer to each question to guide you deeper into the sales process, learning as you go what it is that they want to own.
- **Acknowledge a Fact.** Rather than just stating facts, offer them questions to create engagement. "Did you know that, globally, more than 25 million homes have decentralized solar on their roofs, and by 2030, it's predicted to exceed 100 million? Does knowing that change your thinking about the world's perception of solar power?"
- **Receive Minor Agreements.** Your goal is to get the "yes" momentum going. Even getting buyers to agree it's a beautiful day is a start. When people agree with something you say, it relaxes them, making them more comfortable with you.

- **Arouse and Control Emotions.** Feelings are the gasoline that drives solutions. When you ask a "how do you feel" question and people are comfortable enough to answer, you make tremendous headway in the sales process.
- **Isolate Objections**. This can be as simple as saying, "What, if anything, would prevent you from deciding to go ahead today?"
- **Answer Objections**. Many objections are used just to slow down the sales process. When you hear a real "stall" or hesitation, ask, "If I can prove to you that this product provides a solution for that concern, would you be ready to go ahead?" If the answer is "yes," pull out whatever information you have that proves your product addresses their concern. End with "That answers your concern, doesn't it?" to get their agreement and another "yes" in the forward momentum of the sales process.
- **Keep Buyers Involved.** Selling is a two-way conversation. If it weren't, we would all be lecturers with no Q&A. Even a quick, "Isn't it interesting to learn new information?" can engage a buyer.
- **Gather Information**. This is your qualification sequence. List what you need to know to determine if someone is qualified to own your product, then

write out questions that will guide them to provide that specific information.

- **Solve Problems.** Before tackling a challenge, clarify the underlying issue with questions. Ensure you know everything causing them pain as it relates to your product or situation. Then, ask what their expectations are for a solution. It could very well be that their expectation is far less than you were gearing yourself up to offer.
- **Clarify Your Understanding.** One of my favorite ways to clarify something is to ask for help. Most people respond positively when someone asks for a bit of help. "Mike, would you please help me to understand your situation a little bit better? You have a reason for saying that (whatever comment it was). Would you mind sharing with me?"

Properly placed questions during your sales conversations give you control, provide you with information, and get your potential buyers to tell you precisely what they want to own.

Types of Questions

Now, it's time to cover the types of questions we want to use. Even if you have a degree in communication, like some of the salespeople mentioned at the beginning of the chapter, it's time to think about how to apply what you know strategically.

There are two types of questions that are the staples of sales strategies. Whether you already know of them doesn't matter. What matters is how effective they are when used strategically.

1. Open Questions

   These are questions whose answers require thought on the part of the buyer. They are not yes/no or single-answer questions. We use them to encourage others to share more, open up, elaborate, or clarify something. We learned these in school when we were tasked with writing papers. We had to answer six basic questions to provide complete information. Do you remember? The questions began with Who, What, When, Where, Why, and How. These questions allow you to generate qualitative answers from buyers that are, for the most part, full of information. By asking this type of question, you are allowing them to answer whatever they like. You're still controlling the sales process, but you're giving them the lead position as they perceive it.

   - **Who**, besides yourself, is involved in making buying decisions? The answer to this question tells you whether to give an introductory presentation or your full presentation to the person you're speaking with. If someone else needs to be involved, the sooner you know that and adjust, the better. You may need to switch from presenting to "selling" if others need to be present.

- **What** do you like most about what you have now? The answer here lets you know a few things. First, you can get an idea of the minimum features or benefits they expect from a replacement product. Additionally, you will gain insight into their thoughts and feelings about the product or its benefits. If they are neutral about the product, you will approach it differently than if they are extremely excited.
- **When** were you planning to make a final decision about this purchase? People can be super excited about your product but not have the financial means to own it right now. It may be something that's "in the budget" for next month, next quarter, or next year. You need to know the answer to this to be able to flex or adapt your presentation. The further out the purchase date is in their minds, the more urgency you need to create to close the sale today.

- **Where** in your home/office would you like to have it installed? Never assume every buyer is the same. Even if ninety-nine out of one hundred of your clients had your product installed in the same area, you're bound to encounter someone who wants it done differently. And that difference may not be feasible if your product has specific space or power requirements.

  As a quick example, let's consider a hot water heater. I've seen them in garages, laundry rooms, hall closets, basements, and attics. This question is particularly important for physical products. With an intangible product, your "where" question might be about where to meet with a key contact to implement the product or where to send your invoice.

- **Why** do you feel that is important to your decision? The answer here will often bring about a story about a bad experience the buyer had or heard about. If that story made a major impact on them, you need to acknowledge it and help them resolve their feelings before moving forward in the sales process. The why question might also reveal an absolute need that your product does not resolve. If that's the case, wouldn't you want to know as soon as possible so you don't waste your time and theirs presenting something that won't work for them?

- **How** are you feeling about what I've shared with you so far? Taking the temperature of the buyer partway through the sales process will let you know if it's time to slow down, speed up, or go for the close.

Open questions are so valuable to the practicing sales professional that I suggest you write several questions for each so that you can work them into the flow of your sales process.

2. Closed Questions

   These types of questions are narrow and focused. They could be yes/no questions or require a one-word answer. Use them to prompt buyers to be specific and give clear answers. They can even be used as closing questions. Let's go over a couple.

   a. **Alternate Choice Questions**

      These are "this or that" questions, which suggest two options for the buyer to choose from. The strategy is to offer two options that both move the sale forward. "Shall we schedule delivery for Tuesday or Thursday?" With either answer, installation is moving forward, right? This is a good option for getting buyers to choose features, such as color, by asking questions like, "Do you prefer the blue one or the black one?" or add-ons, by asking, "Are you comfortable with the two-year warranty that comes with it, or would five years make more sense?"

b. Tie-Down Questions

These are the "yes/no" questions. They most often involve contractions, like "doesn't it?", and they typically require a yes or no answer. These types of questions are powerful for starting or adding to the "yes" momentum in your sales process. They are best used when you receive a positive response from your buyer, such as them nodding in agreement to a point you made. This is such a valuable yet straightforward strategy that you'll want to use it frequently. The challenge comes when you use a strategy too often. It becomes evident to the buyer what you're doing, and they may start to fight you. Because of that, I'll cover four types of tie-downs you can intermingle in your sales presentations: Regular, Inverted, Internal, and Tag-on.

- With the **Regular Tie-Down**, the call for an answer is a contraction at the end of a sentence: "It makes sense to replace your roof now before the winter storms begin, doesn't it?" When you say "doesn't it" here, include a slight nod. You are asking for and encouraging agreement.

- An **Inverted Tie-Down** has you place the contraction at the beginning of the question: "Doesn't it make sense to replace your roof now before the winter storms begin?" This is the more direct version of the tie-down.
- The **Internal Tie-Down** is this: "It makes sense, doesn't it, to replace your roof before the winter storms begin?" This version is a bit more conversational. It is likely to be perceived as less direct, a softer version, if you will.
- The **Tag-On** is used when the buyer says something positive about what you're presenting. Buyer: "It makes sense to replace the roof before the winter storms begin." You: "Doesn't it?"

It's worth investing time in writing positive statements and questions for *your* product or service to have ready for your next sales presentation. To practice your delivery of the various questioning strategies, use them in your daily communications with loved ones, friends, and associates.

Get into the habit of asking open questions with everyone and see how your understanding of them expands. Use closed questions for fun topics, such as going out to lunch or dinner. The Alternate Choice question, "Shall we go out for Mexican or Chinese tonight?" is a great one. With either choice, you're going out to eat.

Speaking of practicing with loved ones or associates, here's a simple exercise. It's called "piggybacking." You begin by asking the other person a question. Rather than thinking about what you want to say next—one of the most significant flaws in 90 percent of salespeople—listen for something in their answer that you can acknowledge or comment on. Then, based on what they say, ask another question that makes sense in the context of the communication, yet guides the conversation in the direction you want it to go. Let's say you want to have lunch with someone you've just met. Begin with an open question:

> You: Hey, Jack, I wonder if you can help me. I'm new to the area and am looking for a good place to grab a sandwich for lunch. Where do you usually go?
>
> Jack: I like the subs at the Garden Cafe.
>
> You: The Garden Cafe. I'm not familiar with that one. What do you like best about it?

Jack: The service is quick, and they make their own bread daily.

You: Fresh-made bread. That sounds great. Where is the Garden Cafe located?

Jack: It's a couple of blocks over on 3rd Street, next to the CVS.

You: Third Street, next to the CVS. Thanks. Hey, if you haven't had lunch yet, why not join me? We both need good sustenance for the rest of the day, don't we?

You get the idea. Know your end goal. Then work backward to find the starting point, constantly acknowledging the other person's comments to keep them engaged and steer the conversation toward your goal. Play with this strategy, and you'll soon become a better conversationalist—one with purpose who drives toward a goal. Practicing sales professionals know that the only thing more important than learning the ins and outs of their product is knowing how to ask effective questions to engage and retain buyers.

CHAPTER 11

Opposite/Reverse Selling

A COMPLETED SALE is, in fact, a series of sales. When you first meet people, you are the product. You are selling yourself as a human being who is likeable, interesting, and knowledgeable. You use your energy, excitement, and enthusiasm to persuade others to hear you out. That's your first yes.

That "sale" leads to the next, where you introduce your product through a problem/solution model. When you recognize that they have a need, you ask questions to determine where buyers are on a yes/no scale. It's kind of like the kids' game of hot and cold. When buyers lean in or ask questions about the product, they're getting hotter. They're sliding more to the "yes" side of the scale. When they cross their arms, lean back, or look skeptical, they're getting colder, in essence, moving toward the "no" side of the scale. Your job is to keep the momentum going when it's in favor of "yes" or turn it around when it's trending toward "no."

Being Different

In sales, being different is a good thing. Approaching buyers and talking with them in a way that differs from most salespeople creates a distinct vibe with them. People have expectations of stereotypical salespeople, including what they say and do, how they dress, and how they act. Potential buyers have developed their standard responses to what's expected in sales situations. A prime example of this can be found in retail. We have all heard "May I help you?" when entering a retail environment. And the employee barely gets it out of their mouth before we smile and say, "No, thanks," and keep walking. It's a trite, meaningless non-conversation, and the opportunity to serve is lost.

I love being different. I love coming across as the exact opposite of what buyers expect. I avoid being "salesy" like the plague. A strategy I like to use is to tell buyers early in my presentation that, as I explain the features and benefits of my product, I want them to look for reasons to say no. I say, "In fact, I'm going to help you. Rather than telling you all the success stories about this product, I will give you all the reasons NOT to own it." This is when I really get their attention because this approach is often new to them. It piques their curiosity, and I gain their full attention. Then, during my presentation, I incorporate both the pros and cons of ownership. I'm not pushing anything. I'm simplifying the information like a balance sheet. No tricks. No manipulation.

Alternatively, I might say, "Before I tell you all the reasons this makes sense, I'm going to tell you when it doesn't make sense." This works well to determine how qualified the buyer is for my particular product. When I can list sound reasons they shouldn't go ahead, it's another tick in the win column for building their trust.

When speaking with a potential training buyer, I might tell them they wouldn't want to invest in the training if they don't plan to have everyone on the team go through it. Or if they aren't likely to work with the team to continue implementing it after I leave, it is not a smart purchase. That would be a waste of both time and money. It would demoralize the sales team if the company isn't truly behind the implementation of something I prove works.

As a side note, with this strategy, I don't take on the pressure some salespeople feel to make every sale. Yes, I want to, but I don't ever want to come across as aggressive, manipulative, or pressuring the buyer. My relaxed demeanor transfers to the buyers, and they become more comfortable with me. Being different, in this way, reduces a lot of sales resistance.

The Psychology of Yes and No

There is psychology behind every "yes" and every "no." The yeses can only come through the professional practice of your craft as a salesperson. Your skills will help you build a "yes" momentum that leads to closed sales. Buyers agree to meet you. They agree to hear you out. They agree with some of the things you say. They answer your questions in the affirmative. That's all part of the yes momentum. Of course, there may be a few pauses and negatives between those yeses. However, as long as the "yeses" outweigh the "nos," you should be able to close the sale and, hopefully, get some qualified referrals from them for additional business.

Unpracticed salespeople see "nos" as stop signs or roadblocks. They accept defeat without questioning the psychology behind those "nos." I hate it when I see that happen. The word "no" can carry many meanings, and it can be financially costly for you to assume you know what it means to your buyers. Practicing sales professionals make a study of the word and its many meanings. They prepare themselves to ask questions every time they hear a "no" to determine if there is another approach they can take, more information they can provide, or any number of other solutions we will cover. Here are some of the reasons for saying "no" that I've encountered:

1. Lack of understanding. As I mentioned earlier in the book, a confused mind always says no. If your buyer doesn't see a clear path forward, they will try to stop the momentum of the sale. Any lack of understanding on their part is on you. It's up to you to identify the issue and continue to educate them. Different buyers need different amounts of information or need to have information shared in different ways or with different examples. This is where your highly practiced communication skills come into play. With certain products and buyers, there's a fine line between providing just the right amount of information and information overload. Since information overload almost always leads to a stall of some sort, it's better to deliver information a little at a time and get feed-

back along the way that tells you whether they're ready for more. A few ways to get that feedback are to ask:

a. How are you guys feeling about this so far?
b. Does this sound fair and reasonable?
c. Are you excited about this?
d. Does this all make sense to you?

Feeling out where the buyers are throughout your presentation helps you determine the direction to take next in your presentation or to move ahead to the close.

2. Lingering questions. This is different from a lack of understanding. They may understand what you've shared with them, but have additional questions. Finding that out after they've said "no" can be as simple as asking, "What questions do you have that I have not answered yet?" Using the word "yet" is a subtle way of keeping the process moving, rather than letting their "no" cause a complete stop. For some buyers, the word "no" really means "yes, but . . ." They're interested in the product but haven't yet heard what will make them comfortable enough to make a buying decision.

   Once you've been selling your product for a while, you'll hear the same few questions or concerns repeatedly. They will be your product's lingering questions. When you recognize them, work them right into your presentation to get ahead of them and prevent the most common lingering questions from stalling your sales process. When you bring them up, they often carry less weight with the buyers. "If you're like most of the people I serve, you probably want these three questions answered . . ." Then, answer them. You'll likely diffuse their skepticism. You may also cover material the buyer wasn't aware of yet and needed to know. Either way, you win!

3. A misstep in qualification. Hopefully, you have your qualification questions well-rehearsed, but you will likely encounter buyers whose initial answers are guarded or maybe even untrue. They may not intend to mislead you, but may not answer fully the first time you ask.

   An example might be that the person who identifies themselves as the final decision-maker actually has to present their findings to a team or committee. It could be that the buyer says the product is "in the budget," but the budget is smaller than you expect. Another potential situation is that something in your presentation brings other needs to mind that the product you're presenting doesn't fulfill. It's important to be flexible enough to transition to a different product when this happens, rather than the one presented initially.

4. Lack of trust. This is the bottom-line objection that most of us face. Some buyers may just be skeptical of what you're saying. The offer could seem too good to be true in their minds, which surely would cause them to pause or even initially say "no," not wanting to leap into it too quickly.

   When you sense this, it's usually helpful to be blunt. You might say something like, "Jim, may I have your permission to be blunt with you? I'm not here to play any games or use manipulative practices. I'm being honest about what I see as a real benefit to you. Please level with me, does this offer seem too good to be true? Is that what's holding you back from making a decision?"

5. Timing. You may have the right product, but now is not the right time for the buyer. Maybe they have other priorities ahead of this one. Be prepared to discuss timing options. It could be that their "no" means "not right now." In some of these cases, creating urgency may prompt them to proceed. In others, you may need to follow up with them when they think they'll be ready.

You might say, "I understand you're hesitant, Bob. When do you think you'd like to start having greater peace of mind by owning this product?" Or "Sue, based on all of the benefits we've discussed here tonight, when do you think you would want to take advantage of this program?" Sue might have a large bill due this week or have a reimbursement check coming that she plans to use for this investment. The point is that you can't move the sale forward until you know what is truly holding her back.

The most challenging aspect of door-to-door sales is the timing. We are popping into people's worlds when they have a million other things on their minds or their schedules. If there is a situation where now is not the best time, but they do express interest in your product, say, "The hardest part of my job is timing. I'm just looking for a time that works for both of us to show you the benefits of solar/replacement windows/a new roof. When *is* the best time for you?" And give them a couple of options for you to return.

6. Features. Their "no" might mean "no, not that size or color." When hearing those types of "nos," well-trained salespeople will reflexively ask questions to clarify what the clients mean. They might

say something like, "What preferences (or specifications) have I missed?" Or "If I can get this for you in that size or that color, are you ready to go ahead today?" If they continue to stall, ask, "What needs to happen for you to go ahead and start enjoying the benefits of this product today?" They might jokingly come back with, "You could tell me it's free." If they do that, you know money is the issue. You then keep the sale moving forward by working on financial solutions for them.

7. Not you. With some clients, the "no" you hear could even mean "no, not you." Please note that with some product sales, clients don't just buy the product—they're also buying future involvement with you. In many cases, the salesperson becomes the key connection between the buyer and the company, and they may just not have been "sold" on you. They may not feel comfortable with your ability to serve their needs. You always have to demonstrate your level of competence while demonstrating your product's benefits.

Did this section make you think differently about the word "no"? I hope it did. For me, most often "no" means "know." The buyers need to know more about me, my industry, my product, or the problem I can help them solve. Or I need to know more about their questions and concerns.

Once you understand the many potential meanings of "no," you can prevent it from killing your sales. Instead, you'll take a different approach to the word "no" and keep the sales process moving forward, even if the sale is not meant to happen today.

The Secrets of the Take Away

Just like the sales professionals who learn and master techniques, some buyers will do the same. Sales professionals learn ways to sell. Buyers learn ways to avoid being sold.

When you hear the word "no" and are unable to quickly determine the real reason your buyer said it, I want you to do the opposite of what they expect. This is one of the secrets of the super pros in sales. Buyers expect you to sell harder, to reiterate the benefits of your product, to offer special pricing or free delivery, if applicable. They expect you to either go away or offer them something more. That's what weak, stereotypical salespeople do. I would like you to withdraw the offer. That's right. I want you to back off. This is called the "Take Away" strategy.

If the buyer tells you they don't want your product, respect their choice. Remember, we never want to push anyone into anything. Acting like you're accepting the buyers' "no" and starting to end the sales process will pull them toward the decision if they were saying "no" to see what else you'd offer. With the Take Away, you are, in essence, creating a sense of scarcity in the buyer's mind. It's as if you're saying, "Okay, I don't really care if you do this or not. I'll move on to another buyer." Your attitude is one of "I'm here to serve if you want to take advantage of this. If you want to do it, I can be the one to help you. If you don't, I'll get out of your hair."

Reversing expectations works wonders at knocking down the walls of resistance most people have about salespeople in general. Coming across as different from all the rest catches buyers' attention and builds their curiosity. Opposite/reverse selling is a winning strategy.

CHAPTER 12

Creating the Emotional Climate to Close the Sale

ONE OF THE most important lessons I learned early in my career is that people make buying decisions emotionally. This is not often covered in basic sales training, which is why so many people find sales to be such a challenging job. They believe that if they simply present the facts and demonstrate the benefits of their product, everyone will want to own it.

Earlier in the book, I mentioned that our job is to create emotions in people that cause them to feel comfortable making buying decisions. I'm not trying to change their mind. I'm trying to change their mood.

What I discovered about the typical salesperson is that they try to sell rationally. They fail to evoke emotions or test the emotional temperature of their buyers throughout their presentations, which causes them to struggle to close sales.

The disconnect often occurs in presentations when salespeople fail to link the features of their product to the benefits those features provide to the end user. Most features are tangible—something buyers can feel, smell, taste, see, or measure. The benefits are what those features do for them—how they solve a problem or how they make the buyer *feel.*

For most people, the tipping point of buying decisions is that gut feeling they get after being educated. They understand the problem more clearly because of the knowledge or examples we share. Having a better understanding builds their confidence, allowing them to wisely evaluate potential solutions. Our demonstration of knowledge and understanding of both their problem and how they feel creates confidence in us. When buyers are confident in all three—themselves, us, and our product—the emotional climate is ripe for a sale to be closed.

Creating Curiosity is Critical

To sell, the primary objective is to create curiosity in the buyer's mind. We do that by being likable and making the product information make sense. If buyers are not curious, they will not be interested. When I hear them say, "We're not interested." It's nothing more than an objection, a reflex they've made a habit of using. It's most often a smokescreen to deter the average salespeople.

When I hear "We're not interested," I make it my job to blow that screen away. I start by acknowledging it. I say something like, "I understand. Of course, you don't want to buy anything right this second," and just keep going forward by trying to build their curiosity.

Objections Are Just Another Part of the Sales Process

An objection is a tactic used by buyers to stall or prolong a final decision. They have techniques. We have techniques. One of two things is going to happen in every sales process:

1) My level of belief is going to be higher, and I'm going to move forward in the sales process.
2) Their resolve will be stronger than mine, and they will stop the sales process entirely.

When buyers are in resistance mode, they are looking for every reason to say "no." It's your job to give them every reason to say "yes."

What Is Closing?

Closing is the act of creating the actual purchase decision. It's really that simple. It's the end of the sales presentation and the conversion of the relationship. The "buyer" is no longer a buyer; they are becoming a client or one of the "people we serve." Closing is that magical transition point.

To be more creative with the description, Tom Hopkins defines closing as "a symphony of words and actions that culminates in a win-win final decision." I love the concept of what we do as creating or leading a symphony—blending facts and building emotions to a harmonious crescendo. We blend the facts, information, and logic of the presentation with words that evoke an emotional connection, creating a sense of ownership where the buyer feels compelled to choose our product, making the decision a no-brainer and leaving them relieved or pleased to do so. *Relief* might be the emotion they feel when they realize the solution to their problem is being actualized. *Pleased* would be the emotion they experience when the purchase "just feels right." They feel *smart* and *happy* that they're buying it.

Once we use the words that create feelings of desire to own our offering, our buyers will defend their feelings with logic. Our job, then, is twofold:

1. First, say and do the right things to create those feelings.
2. Then, present the logical reasons for moving forward.

The Checkpoints Necessary to Closing

As we covered in Chapter 10, the application of effective questioning strategies is the starting point for closing. It's where we gain the information needed to determine how to move forward in the sales process and which product the buyers will most likely want to own. But there's more to it than that. We use practical questions in every step of the sales process. Here's what a sample standard sales process might look like:

Prospecting → Making an Initial Contact
→ Qualifying/Determining Need
→ Presenting or Demonstrating the Product
→ Addressing Concerns or Overcoming Objections
→ Closing the Sale

As you can see, a lot needs to happen before we get to closing. I like to use boxing as an analogy for closing. It's not that we throw punches or "pitches" (that nasty word was covered in Chapter 2). Not at all. We don't wear our opponents down. When boxers like Mike Tyson and Mohammed Ali won fights, when did it usually happen? Rarely in the first round. And even more rarely with a single punch. Most boxers win with combinations as setups for the big punch. It's the same thing in sales.

With most buyers, it will take several instances of saying "no" before the tipping point is reached, where we finally get the "yes." J. Douglas Edwards, also known as the Father of Modern Day Selling and arguably the pioneer of sales training, used to say that the reason there is so much mediocrity within the sales field is that most salespeople only know one or two ways to close sales or, as I like to say, to break the buyers' preoccupation with fear or hesitation to make a commitment. They learn one or maybe two closing sentences, and when they don't work, they assume it's the buyer's fault that they didn't make the sale. Saying things like, "So, do you want to move to the next step?" can be a sales killer, yet many salespeople continue to use it as their default close. It's no wonder they're not making sales.

Practicing sales professionals master multiple techniques for moving from addressing concerns to closing sales. They know them so well that they can flex from one to another smoothly. To continue with the boxing analogy, salespeople need to stay "light on their feet." They need to be ready to flex in any direction the buyers' input shows them, while staying focused on what the next "yes" will be. You can't reflex an idea. You have to reflex the techniques. It's what separates the average from the great in sales.

There may be times when the salesperson encounters unanticipated resistance and needs to back away, changing the angle of approach or even briefly changing the subject to relieve any perceived pressure on the buyer. I've done this by asking the buyer an off-topic question about their favorite sports team. This moves their focus to a subject they're comfortable discussing. I can see them visually relax. Then, I'll move back onto the path of the sales process by looking at my sales aids again, pointing to something, or handing them to the buyer. I've even used analogies that involve their team to draw them back into the sales process. Sports and sales share many similarities.

The Number One Hidden Objection

Want to know the number one hidden objection that buyers don't want to share with you? It's this: "It sounds too good to be true." Rarely will a buyer admit this, but it'll be in the back of their mind. What's happening is that everything you've done or said is lining up too quickly or too easily for them. They start to second-guess themselves and want to slow the process. When this happens, here's what I say: "Mike, the bottom line here is that you'll fall into one of two categories: Category 1 is that everything I just explained makes complete and total sense. You may even know somebody who has gotten involved with this product and is happy with it. In Category 2, this just sounds way too good to be true, and you're probably sitting there thinking, 'Wait a second. What's the catch?' The point is, there is no catch when it comes to this product."

At that point, I have their full attention, and I'm like a boxer. I'm "putting them into the corner." With roofing buyers, I might say this next, "What was the main reason that you guys got home insurance in the first place? If you're like the other homeowners we serve, it was so you would have financial coverage if you had legitimate damage, right?" I get a "yes" every time. And that "yes" leads to my team checking out the roof to determine if there is enough damage to file a claim.

With other clients, using this technique usually causes them to relax and admit that purchasing my product is a no-brainer—that some things can be "too good to be true," and it's wise to take advantage of them when they come along.

What Keeps Salespeople from Closing?

All that's holding salespeople back from becoming sales professionals is procrastination. They put off taking the necessary steps to become a practicing sales professional. They don't try to analyze what they're saying, testing, or trying differently.

Procrastination is a career killer. It ruins your future by causing you to avoid the present and live in the past, where you still dreamed of having a "killer" sales career. Dreams cannot become reality when you allow procrastination to enter your life or career. Understand now that procrastination is nothing more than indecision. It can generate anxiety or fear. When those emotions dominate, you won't be able to do what it takes to create buying emotions in others. So, commit to exchanging procrastination with practice, and you'll start closing more sales.

CHAPTER 13

Sales Closing: Power Phraseology

THERE ARE TWO basic types of closings: oral closings and written closings. Which do you think is more important? Tom Hopkins believes that oral closing is more important because the buyer is stating their belief that proceeding makes sense. And I agree. This goes back to Tom's teaching of "when they say it, it's true." Then, you simply move to the paperwork.

Some sales professionals believe nothing is final until it's written. They think that a written closing is more important because the transaction is complete when you get their "approval on the paperwork."

In some types of sales, you cannot have one without the other.

Knowing When to Go for the Close

Developing your instinct for when buyers are ready to make a final decision is one of the most important skills in sales. When you hear buyers speak about your product as if they already own it, they're likely ready to go ahead. When you encounter buyers who keep their opinions to themselves, you'll need to draw them out with questions. Questions for determining how close you are to getting their approval are called test or trial closes. These are open-ended, opinion-seeking questions. Here are two examples:

- "So, how are you feeling about all of this so far?"
- "What aspect of this opportunity gets you most excited?"

When their responses to test or trial closes are positive, there's often no need to close further because the odds that they're going to go ahead are high. Their anxiety is low. When they hesitate to respond, you may need to slow down the sales process or encourage them to tell you what's holding them back or what their concern or objection might be.

Expect "Nos"

Unless the buyer has approached you with an interest in your product, you will likely hear several "nos" during the sales process. Understand that most of those "nos" are their reaction to feeling pulled toward owning your product. Buyers may feel compelled to slow things down, especially in situations where you approach them with a product they hadn't ever considered owning. I have found that most of those objections aren't really objections, and I don't let them stop me. In fact, I only pause briefly to acknowledge that I heard them by saying, "Yeah, that's the thing." Then, I keep moving forward with my presentation. Often, the following few points I cover will eliminate that concern altogether.

If they bring it up again, I know I need to address it. That's when I say, "Obviously, you have a reason for saying that. Would you mind sharing it with me?" This question is great at drawing out more information about their concern. Allowing them space to discuss whatever is giving them pause often causes them to realize it's not a real objection. If it *is* a real objection, I now know specifically what to address. Memorize those two sentences and start using them when buyers hesitate. You will be pleasantly surprised by how effective they are.

Seven Proven Closing Strategies

In my experience, there are no magic words that work every time or with every buyer to close the sale. In this, I agree with J. Douglas Edwards, who believed that to be a sales professional, you have to know many ways of approaching that final agreement and know them so well that you can flex from one to another depending on each situation and type of buyer. He taught that most buyers will say "no" at least five times before they say "yes." So, his advice was that every salesperson needed to know more than five ways to close the sale.

I'll give you seven different sales closes in this chapter. Think about how they feel to you as you read them. Then, reread them, thinking about some of the people you serve and how they might respond. The goal of this exercise is for you to identify the types of buyers who are likely to respond positively to each strategy and those who are not. Then, work on memorizing the words so you can apply the closes appropriately, as needed.

1. *Triplicate of Choice Close*

   I think we've all heard the story about Goldilocks and the Three Bears. Goldilocks was found well-fed and sleeping comfortably after trying things that were too hot, too cold, too hard, and too soft. She found her happy medium. I know that's a fairy tale, but it's the way a lot of us find what's "just right" for us. The number one need of all humans is to be comfortable. As sales professionals, our job is to create that comfortable feeling for buyers so they will make those buying decisions.

With the Triplicate of Choice, we give our buyers three options on the path to a closed sale. The three options help us narrow down what they will find acceptable and feel comfortable owning. The three options include:

- One option that's slightly more than you think they want
- One option that's slightly less than you think they want
- One option that you believe will be the right choice for them

It's important to be cautious about the wording so as not to make them think that you feel they can't afford the high-end or that they'd be settling for the least. Here's an example:

"Sarah, based on what you've shared with me so far, we have three options for the solution to your needs. Most people who decide to own this product go with the medium-sized package. A fortunate few will choose to go with the largest package, and then there are those with a fixed or limited budget who go for the smallest package. Which category do you feel most comfortable with?"

Let's analyze what happens with each choice. If Sarah chooses the middle package, you've made a sale of what you feel is just right for her situation. Yay for you! If she goes with the largest package, it's even better for both of you. If she chooses the smallest package, you have still gained Sarah as a client by making a sale. The key to the success of this strategy is not to recommend anything that doesn't serve her needs well. If any of the three possible options are selected, you've made a sale. Sarah feels she's been given choices and is driving the decision. She *feels* comfortable.

You can use the same strategy with the dollar value of your product, not just with the packages of products. If using it with money, you would begin with an amount about twenty percent above what you expect them to invest in your product. The "fortunate few" amount would be fifty to one hundred percent higher than that. The amount for "those on a budget" would be the actual amount you expect them to be prepared and willing to spend.

This strategy works well with people you feel are middle-of-the-roaders, which is the most significant percentage of people you are likely to encounter.

2. *Secondary Question Close*

   This close is a perfect example of benefiting from the "yes" momentum. The close works like this: You pose the major decision—ask for the sale—but before the buyer has a chance to answer, you ask another question ("secondary") that you are certain they will respond to positively. It might sound like this: "As I see it, Ms. Franklin, the only decision you have to make today is how soon you'll start seeing improved efficiency in your business with this product. By the way, will we be training your entire team at once, or should we plan to train several small groups?"

   What happens next? Ms. Franklin has been asked to decide how she'll handle the training *after* a purchase has been made. When she answers the second question, the answer to the first can be assumed. After all, she wouldn't decide when or how to handle training if she wasn't planning on going ahead. Your next step would be to confirm training dates and get her approval on the paperwork.

This close could almost be called the "Skip Close" as you skip forward, assumptively, to what needs to happen next.

3. *I Want to Think About It*, also known as *The Everything I Said Close*

   When you have done your job well in determining a buyer's needs and demonstrated how your product is the perfect solution, the buyer may feel that things are moving relatively quickly. They may start to think, "Can it be this easy to find a good solution?" or "Is this too good to be true?" What happens next is that most buyers will say something like "I want to think about it" to stall or slow down the buying momentum. They'll start to second-guess their thinking. It's a perfectly normal reflex.

   Average salespeople will hear the stall, believe it to be a hard "no," and give up on even trying to close the sale. The practicing sales professional knows this reflex means it's time for a pause, a recap, or a summary of what's been covered. It means the buyer is leaning toward making the purchase but needs to reaffirm they're making the right decision.

   So, how do we handle this stall respectfully? We pause. We agree with them by saying, "That's fine," "I see," or "I understand." Then, we ask more questions. It goes like this, "Obviously, you wouldn't take your time thinking this over unless you were seriously interested, would you?" Wait for their "yes." Then, we confirm what they've said. "Since you're indicating that you're interested, may I assume you'll give it very careful consideration?" Wait for another "yes." They'll give it because now they think you're going to leave.

Now, we give them opportunities to say "no," but these "nos" mean "yes."

"Just to clarify my thinking, what is it you wanted to think over?" (Don't pause. List what you've already covered that they liked.) "Is it the reputation of my company?" "No." "Is it me? Did I do or say something wrong?" "No." "Is it the capability of the product?" "No, we agreed it meets our specs." "Is it the color, the design, the delivery date, the installation process, the training...?" (Whatever specs/benefits they already liked).

This close allows you to reiterate or summarize all the benefits they liked during the presentation and narrow down the real reason they're hesitant. After all, few buyers would take the time to reconsider everything at another time or with another person. It's a waste of their precious time. In most cases, stalls like this are because of the money, but you need them to tell you that—point blank—before you can help them rationalize it. End your summary with, "If everything we covered makes sense, may I ask, could your hesitation be the money?" When they say it is, you can focus your efforts on coming up with terms that feel comfortable to them and rationalizations about how the sooner they own your product, the sooner they'll start saving money, being more efficient and productive, or whatever your solution leads to.

4. *The Sharp Angle Close*

   This close is short and to the point. You use it in response to a buyer's question about your product. When the buyer asks, "Does the product do X?" you respond with, "If it did, would you be ready to move forward today?" When they respond with a "yes," and your product does "X," the next thing you do is reach for the "paperwork" and hand it to them for "approval."

   You wouldn't use this close too early in your sales process. Don't skip steps from qualifying to closing unless your buyer is already very familiar with your product.

5. *The Trust Close*

Use this when you feel the buyer is slowing down the process or if their body language is saying they don't trust what you're telling them. It might be as simple as crossing their arms or leaning back in their chair.

Trust is an emotion, and in some cases, you will need to get the buyer to admit they're not feeling comfortable. You may need to get them to rationalize the facts presented before they get comfortable with the emotion that's tied to making a decision.

With this type of buyer, say this, "Sir, the biggest concern I need to help people overcome when considering owning my product is trust. They're not sure if what I'm saying is true. All I can say to that is, if you're willing to give me one percent of your trust today, I'm willing to earn the other ninety-nine as we go, and I'm confident that I will earn it. If we took all the emotion out of the equation and this was a straight-up logical decision based on everything we covered, you would go ahead, wouldn't you?" (Nod) "If you commit to the first step, I will take care of the rest. I'm asking you to put your best foot forward today so we can put you in a more economical position. If you can pay less on a bill that you will never cancel (solar, electric, phone, etc.), there's really no way we can hurt your situation."

6. *Feel, Felt, Found*

   This closing strategy was popularized by the great Zig Ziglar. It's easy to remember and very effective. Using these three words, you acknowledge your buyers' feelings of concern or doubt and reinforce the positive aspects of your offering. Here's what this close sounds like: "I understand how you *feel*, Robert. Some of my other clients *felt* the same way when considering this product, but here's what they *found* after deciding to go ahead." You would then reiterate the positive benefits of going ahead. This is a great closing line to use in your role as an assistant buyer. Understanding how they feel places you on their side. When you discuss what others have *found*, it's those others who are encouraging ownership. You will not be perceived as a pushy salesperson.

7. *Reverse Closing*

   Their excuse becomes their reason. "That's why you should move forward. You don't need it; your loved ones do." Bypass an excuse to say no and continue.

If they bring it up again, say, "That's exactly why you should do it." For example, if some says, "We are moving," I might say, "Exactly, that's why you should do it as this will increase the value of your property and make your home more desirable to a buyer."

Steps to Use After You Use a Close and It Does Not Work

As I mentioned before, not every close will work in every situation. And sometimes, you may need to use several closes before buyers are ready to make a decision. Closing can ebb and flow. You go for the close. They hesitate, stall, or object. You then need to build a bridge to another close. Here's how:

Step 1 - Apologize.

Step 2 - Summarize the benefits with tie-downs. "You did like the fact that (benefit), didn't you?"

Step 3 - Ask your leading question. "I understand that it may seem like we're moving kind of fast, but those are things we have kind of agreed upon, haven't we?"

Step 4 - Move to the next close.

I don't know if I've ever closed a sale on the first try. What matters most is that we don't stop selling when we know our product will truly serve their needs. We simply switch gears and work to create another opportunity to close with a different approach.

The value in the closes given here is that they have been proven to work by other sales professionals and by me within the last few years. That's because they make sense. They follow a specific trail from the buyer's hesitation to rationalization and the decision to own your product.

I urge you to read them a minimum of six times to get comfortable with the wording. Do it six more times, and they will begin to come to you naturally as needed. When you can smoothly deliver them, you will gain the benefit of closing more sales.

CHAPTER 14

The Golden Pearls: Lessons I've Learned Selling

I MAKE IT a habit to frequently reflect on the lessons that have proven most valuable to my overall success so far. I am still in the early days of my sales training career, yet I feel I've lived a couple of lifetimes already in the world of selling. In this chapter, I'll share the gems of knowledge that have meant the most to me thus far. My awareness of them has brought me both success and fulfillment. I call them my "Golden Pearls."

Pearl #1 - Conduct business with people you want to do life with.

When you surround yourself with good, like-minded people, those with similar drive, energy, and passion, every aspect of business improves and carries over into your personal life. The good times and good feelings you share will significantly surpass the earnings. You may not remember exactly how much you earn along the way, but you will remember who you did it with. Your closest associates will always have the greatest impact on you.

This can be considered from two perspectives:

1. If you're working for others at a company that you do not own, pay attention to whether your interactions with leadership, management, and fellow associates lift you or generate tension in you. What are your thoughts on working there? If you love your product, how the company serves its clients, and how it respects its staff, you'll likely want to stay long-term. Note that people do not quit companies. They quit leadership. If you experience tension or disrespect from others within the organization, it won't matter how much you love the product or service; you won't want to stay in that environment.

2. If you're working for yourself or are a leader in a company, ask yourself if you appreciate those around you. Do you demonstrate how they can succeed and grow to achieve higher levels and greater success? Without good leadership, companies perish. Many practicing sales professionals will eventually find themselves in leadership positions. When that happens, it's vital to apply the same level of focused dedication to becoming a great leader that you used to become a top salesperson. Those you lead or manage have become the "people you serve."

The three most important things in any business relationship are trust, loyalty, and longevity. Trust must come first. If I don't trust you, there's no way you will earn my loyalty. All parties involved need to be aligned with the mission if a business, yours or another, is to succeed in the long term. When you surround yourself with people you want to do life with, you increase your odds of long-term success.

Pearl #2 - Next to the word "success" is the word "sacrifice."

This is a really simple concept. If you want something bad enough, you'll make sacrifices to get it.

When I started my first job, I was completely myopic. By "myopic," I mean that I was constantly focused on achieving immediate or short-term results. I had tunnel vision and no distractions. The way I see it, I was emotionally unavailable for anything outside of selling. I even worked all day on my birthday. What could I do at each moment to make it a positive experience for both myself and my clients? I was singularly focused on the matter at hand.

I constantly asked myself, "What could I do differently to get the most out of each day?" What I gained from this perspective was to eliminate distractions. I never let myself get pulled off course with what is called "shiny object syndrome." I evaluated every new piece of information or opportunity against my current tasks and goals. If they didn't fit my plan, I would let them fall away.

My focus remained on continually asking myself this question: "What must I do to get to the next level of success?" Sometimes, the answers were so simple that they surprised me. Other days, they required more thought or action on my part. The hard part comes when it takes longer than you expect.

When I teach people who are highly motivated to achieve new levels of success, I tell them to reflect on what they're doing now that is likely holding them back.

I tell them to figure out what their "kryptonite" is and then figure out what they can do to avoid it.

Your weaknesses interfere with the clarity of your conviction. I believe most adults have created "to-do" lists. They are typically filled with little details that need to be taken care of within a single day, a week, or a month. I'd like to suggest you do the opposite. I want you to write "not-to-do" lists. You know the type of thinking and activities that hold you back from achieving the next level of success. Keep that "not-to-do" list handy, and when you realize you're leaning toward any of your weaknesses, use the opposite/reverse thinking strategies from Chapter 5 to turn yourself around.

An example of this is when you want to eat healthy, but you keep going down the snack aisle at the grocery store. Wouldn't it be smarter to avoid that aisle altogether? Maybe your kryptonite is watching mindless television shows or listening to true crime podcasts instead of taking in knowledge that helps you get smarter about how to achieve your goals and feel more motivated to take action. Don't mistake my advice here for being strong all the time. Be vulnerable but not to your vices. Vulnerability is the birthplace of innovation.

Become your own research and development (R&D) department. R&D is critical for forward progress. And you do have the time for this when you sacrifice the things that aren't moving you forward. What are you willing to sacrifice to gain success? Make that list!

Pearl #3 - First comes the action; then comes the motivation.

Those who live in mediocrity wait to feel motivated to take the next steps toward success. Those who achieve the most in life don't wait. They make moves, then catch the positive vibes those moves create. Operating this way can be exhilarating. It can give you the energy and power you need to continue. It also helps you develop your leadership skills. The first level of leadership is to lead yourself.

It's a lot easier to act and then wait for the motivation to come, rather than waiting for the motivation to strike before you act. I've met a lot of people who get hung up on their "wishbones." They waste their time wishing things were better and feeling unmotivated.

Then, there are the "knucklebones." These are the people who don't train. In some cases, they're lazy, but in other cases, they don't think they need it; they believe training is a waste of time. They won't pick up a book to learn more. They make excuses to avoid training sessions.

They don't understand that every presentation that doesn't lead to a sale *is* training. It's practice, but they're not paying attention to whether they are practicing the wrong things.

There are those whom I refer to as being "jawbones." They talk a good game but rarely take action.

Next are those I refer to as "tail bones." They are at the bottom of the sales pile. The only actions they take are getting ready to take action, looking busy, but never actually taking action. They don't last long in this business.

And then there are what I call the "Pop-Tart" salespeople. They want to "microwave" their success. They spend all their energy looking for shortcuts.

The most successful people I've met rely on their backbones. They don't hesitate to act on their thoughts, to keep going, and create opportunities. They understand that thoughts yield *potential* power, but it is action that produces *real* power.

Pearl #4 - Have fun!

Instead of judging your success based on the number of sales made each day or how big a sale is, rate yourself on a scale of one to ten in these areas:

- What was your level of effort and input for the day? How much time did you spend in situations where you could close sales?
- How interest*ing* and interest*ed* were you? To create interest, you have to be interested. Create curiosity. Curiosity creates interest.
- How much fun did you have? If none, this job isn't worth it. If you're having fun getting rejected because you know how to use opposite/reverse thinking as covered in Chapter 5, give yourself high marks.

The higher your ratings in these areas, the more sales you'll make. When you start stacking up thirty-point days, you're going to get sales. You have control over each of these three areas. Maximize what you're doing with each.

Pearl #5 - The harder I work, the luckier I get.

This is all about work ethic. It's likely that you have already developed a set of values, beliefs, and behaviors around your approach to work. They are your compass to use as a point of reference for your thoughts and actions.

I remember when I was sixteen, and my dad dropped me off at the orientation for my job as a golf caddy. There were twenty others at that same orientation. Yet, walking up to the first hole, I had an "aha" moment that I would be the best caddy in the whole group. I believed this was a job I could excel at, even though I'd never done it before. My attitude made me stand a little taller and walk with confidence. At that time, I didn't even know that people judge your level of confidence and competence based on your walk. It just felt like the right thing for the "best caddy" to do.

You know in your gut if you're not giving it your all. If you're not getting the results that you want out of life or from your sales career, your compass might need a reset.

Look around at others who are achieving what you want to achieve. Consider the values and behaviors they demonstrate and decide if yours need adjusting. Remind yourself often of your vision, and you'll be more motivated to do the work necessary to achieve it.

Pearl #6 - We all get energy from "Yes."

I equate this to collecting mushrooms in the Mario video games. The more you get, the more you want to play, right?

Close your eyes and think, right now, about the last "yes" you got. Do you feel how your energy rises when you replay it in your mind? Are you standing taller or sitting up straighter in your chair? Our bodies respond to what our brains think. To create more energy in your body, mentally relive a powerful "yes" moment. Do this several times each day and watch what happens. When you control how you think, you will be better able to transfer your energy to others, influencing how they think.

Pearl #7 - When we teach others, we are practicing and performing sales transactions at our highest level.

I believe we should all find someone to teach or mentor. That's because when we do, we are practicing our skills and giving it our best. After all, we want others to learn the best of what we have to offer.

When I am hired to train sales teams, I don't just lecture. I go into the field with them and sell their product to genuine live buyers I've never met before. Yes, I also do classroom teaching, but the most significant benefit I bring to them is going beyond in-house role-playing to real-life demonstrations, where none of us knows what will happen next. Not many sales trainers are willing to take that risk, but it's what keeps me sharp as both a salesperson and a teacher. Find someone to mentor or, at the very least, work with a fellow sales professional on improving each other's skills.

Pearl #8 - We get better or worse all the time. There is no neutral in sales or life.

This can be a tough one to accept at first, but it really makes sense. The great Notre Dame football coach, Lou Holtz, said, "Nothing on this earth is standing still. It's either growing or dying." I agree with him 100 percent.

Staying in our comfort zone is the worst thing we can allow. I think you'll agree with me that some of the most exhilarating moments in our lives are when we take major leaps forward, ending up with opportunities that are entirely outside our comfort zones. Risk is the down payment for success. Sometimes we need to commit now and figure it out later. With a lot of the goals I set and achieved, I didn't really believe I could accomplish them in the beginning. However, as I took the first steps, the next steps I needed to achieve them became clearer. Set goals that scare you a bit because they will be fertilizer for your growth. They will shift you into "getting better" mode, and soon you'll find the challenge exciting.

Pearl #9 - The real currency of life is relationships, not money.

Sales can be a lonely business. When it's likely we will face rejection on a daily basis, it's important to have people in our corner who will lift us. It's those people we will celebrate the highs with. That's why it's important to include your loved ones in your career journey. When we have others with whom we enjoy the rewards of our hard efforts, it doubles the fun!

Pearl #10 - Temporary imbalance is how you will get ahead.

When companies need to increase sales, they often organize sales blitzes to generate a specific dollar amount or to sell larger quantities of a particular product. Doing so, either through your company or independently, requires a significant amount of time and effort. It can take a toll, both mentally and emotionally.

Enter these periods with the understanding that the required imbalance is temporary. Gear yourself up prior to launching into a blitz so you can put forth that extra work, but keep in mind that it's temporary. Once the dollar amount or time frame is achieved, you *will* come back into balance, refresh, and recharge yourself.

Ninety-nine percent of people can't do what we do. They just don't have the mental mindset for sales. We think differently. We understand that we need to operate in run-rest cycles, especially if the products we sell have seasonal selling cycles. I want you to understand, though, that it's unhealthy to run hard all the time. You will wear out or burn out. When planning each month's activities, include time to rest, recover, and recharge so you can handle those temporary imbalances well.

Pearl #11- Each presentation needs to be personalized to the location and buyer.

I mentioned earlier in the book the importance of using "first-time" energy with buyers, even though you may have given your presentation a thousand times. Implementing this pearl will help you with that. If buyers feel you are operating on autopilot, they won't be any more interested in what you're saying than you are. When you personalize every presentation, you'll be more interest*ing,* and they'll be more interest*ed.* You'll be able to personalize it to suit Mr. & Mrs. Jones, who live in a Florida retirement community on a fixed income, or match Mr. Parker, the corporate purchasing agent in Chicago, with a multi-million-dollar budget and twelve departments to serve. When you focus on personalization, you find ways to put yourself in their shoes, to, in essence, sit on their side of the table.

Pearl #12 - Pay attention to the scoreboard.

At the very least, every week, take stock of where you are on the achievement of your sales goals and your personal goals. By paying attention to the scoreboard, you can make minor adjustments to what you are learning or doing. If you pay attention to the scoreboard, the scoreboard will pay attention to you. When you don't pay attention, the required adjustments may become major, even causing an interruption in your forward progress or a break in a relationship.

I keep this list of pearls readily accessible on my phone. I refer to it frequently to keep my mind, attitude, and business on the path I've chosen. I highly recommend you do the same.

CONCLUSION

The Main Thing is to Keep the Main Thing the Main Thing

EARLY IN THE book, I mentioned the value of having clarity around what you want, what you are working for, and how you will work to get it. Clarity is the starting point of everything. In fact, there's a path for achieving success that goes like this:

> Clarity creates conviction. Conviction creates belief. Belief creates energy. Your energy creates repetition. The repetition creates service. Your service creates your life's work. Your life's work creates freedom.

I believe the ultimate goal of every living person is freedom. How you define that is up to you. It might be financial freedom. It might be time freedom. It might be location freedom, where you don't "have to" be in any one place at a given time. You can travel all you want, or you can plant yourself in the middle of a deserted island or even in your favorite neighborhood. You choose. With freedom, you are literally not tied to anything. Can you even imagine that? I hope you can because nothing compares to that feeling of freedom. And that emotion will carry you forward to great success in the field of sales.

Everything you are doing when you are not in direct communication with a buyer should be to get you into the groove when you are. The reason I was able to get to the top at all the companies I worked for was that I had absolute clarity about what I wanted, which created in me a certainty about winning. Losing was not an option. I cut out all of my distractions. I was completely myopic. I understood the key element to my success would be to keep the main thing the main thing.

Sure, there were times when I was tempted to veer off the path I set for myself. There were days when quitting early and going home for a nap sounded so good. There will be days like that again. But I choose not to give in, give up, or get distracted. I want what I want so strongly, so *ardently*, that I won't let anything get in my way. I keep my main thing as my main thing. With laser focus on my endgame, I know I will win.

ASK THE AUTHOR

Ask the Author is your opportunity to use AI designed to answer your toughest questions with answers straight from Taylor McCarthy.

Give him your toughest objections and discover the perfect response.

Using this tool, you'll add new sales skills to your quiver in no time. Learn how to counter objections like Taylor, one of the top closers in the business.

Try it out! Here are a couple ideas to get this party started:

- Give it your last objection to see how Taylor would respond.
- Record your entire sales pitch, either in person or virtual. Post call, get a report with detailed advice on your pitch.

"After training millions of sales professionals worldwide for over fifty years, I've finally found the person to carry on the torch to the generations to come."
—Tom Hopkins, bestselling author of *How to Master the Art of Selling*

How to Master the Art of Selling 2

WINNING THE GAME OF SALES

TAYLOR McCARTHY

FOREWORD BY TOM HOPKINS

Give it a try today!

"Using Ask the Author just four times, I learned new skills in countering the toughest sales objections in my industry. Mind bender!"

Bryan Heathman, former Xerox Sales Executive

ABOUT THE AUTHOR

TAYLOR McCARTHY IS a seasoned sales expert, international speaker, and author with more than eighteen years of experience, including his own record-setting sales record and helping sales teams optimize their strategies to grow revenue.

Taylor gained national recognition for door-to-door sales in the solar and security industries. He achieved the honor of Direct Sales Person of the Year for three consecutive years in his field.

His practical, results-producing sales skills have made him a frequent speaker at industry conferences. He is also the founder of Knockstar University, created to improve the skills of door-to-door sales teams.